Complexity and Enterprise Systems
Engineering

TOWARD SOLVING COMPLEX
HUMAN PROBLEMS

Complex and Enterprise Systems Engineering

Series Editors: Dr. Paul R. Garvey of The MITRE Corporation and Dr. Brian E. White of CAU-SES (Complexity Are Us—Systems Engineering Strategies)

These books represent evolving perceptions of complexity, complex systems, and complex systems engineering, including those associated with most systems, system of systems, and enterprises. One of the most recent characteristics and advocated guidelines is to intentionally and inherently include all the key stakeholders as integral components of the system being developed or improved.

For more information about this series, please visit: https://www.routledge.com/Complex-and-Enterprise-Systems-Engineering/book-series/AUECOMENTSYS

TOWARD SOLVING COMPLEX HUMAN PROBLEMS

Techniques for Increasing Our Understanding of What Matters in Doing So

Brian E. White

CRC Press
Taylor & Francis Group
Boca Raton London New York

CRC Press is an imprint of the
Taylor & Francis Group, an **informa** business

Problem
Approaches
Architecture
Alternatives
Solutions
Contingencies
Implementations
Capabilities
Effectiveness

C & E S E

First edition published 2021
by CRC Press
6000 Broken Sound Parkway NW, Suite 300, Boca Raton, FL 33487-2742

and by CRC Press
2 Park Square, Milton Park, Abingdon, Oxon, OX14 4RN

© 2021 Taylor & Francis Group, LLC

CRC Press is an imprint of Taylor & Francis Group, LLC

ISBN: 978-0-367-63848-1 (hbk)
ISBN: 978-1-003-12098-8 (ebk)

Typeset in Times New Roman
by MPS Limited, Dehradun

To
Beverly Gay McCarter

In humble recognition of Bev's past but significant and forward-looking contributions to our studies of complexity, complex systems, and complex systems engineering, particularly her artistic and cogent insights concerning people and human minds.

Contents

Foreword

Today you can hardly read about a disaster without hearing about complexity. When nearly any human-made system fails, complexity is named as one of the causes. The Boeing 737 Max flew for three years before it was recognized that some of the alterations made when they increased the length of the fuselage could lead, and have led, to fatal accidents. The multi-year grounding of the entire fleet starting in March 2019, while seeking improvements to make such a complex system safe, has been extraordinarily costly, not only for Boeing but for the airlines that fly the aircraft and for passengers and their organizations.

Today's software-enabled and highly technological systems are so interrelated and so highly coupled that even small irregularities have the potential to cause anything from cost and schedule problems to major disasters. However, these systems exist because they also can do great good. Today, we can check on the status of distant dangerous systems without leaving our desks. Our medical systems automatically alert our doctors to possible problems in our x-rays. We can attend work meetings all day long without leaving our virus-free homes.

As a society, how can we continue to take advantage of the benefits of extreme high technology without suffering the consequences of high complexity? Clearly, we must understand what complexity is; how it works; how it can be controlled in engineering; and, more importantly, how we should bring our understanding into our business enterprises and into society at large for mutual benefit.

This book is an excellent short introduction to this immensely important topic. Are "complex systems" just more complicated than your average systems? No, they are actually different in some important ways, and because of that, we need to engineer them somewhat differently. If we don't, we won't be able to build systems that work right in an efficient manner. And if we do learn to build them well, we can get a lot more capability out of them and it can make our business and our society much better, much more effective, and more ecologically safe as well.

The uniqueness of this book lies in its third chapter. Nothing else I've seen addresses how to move from the engineering and business aspect to the societal aspect. Authors generally focus on the business and smaller (engineering) or the business and larger (society), but not both. Brian's unique ability to tie the two together is what will make you think and take you from this one small guidebook out into a new perspective.

I first met Brian when I joined the Complex Systems Working Group (which he headed) of INCOSE, the International Council on Systems Engineering. After 30 years in engineering, I had begun my doctoral work on systems engineering and complexity and was interested in his work that took systems engineering out of the mechanical, "connect part A to part B" realm into the larger realm, that of "how is this going to work in this complex world in which we live?"

Brian's work opened my eyes to the direct application of complementary "complex systems processes" that add to more typical engineering processes to build more capable systems in an evolutionary manner that adapt in a changing ecosystem of engineered and human systems.

Whether you are an engineer, a businessperson, a journalist, or anyone else interested in the intersection of technology and society, you as a reader will be able to see how to extend the use of engineering tools to address larger, society-based issues. Brian provides a plethora of examples of people who have done this to make our world better and many references you can go to for more information.

I plan to keep this book on hand as I head full steam into my own retirement. After all, now is the time I get to pick the problems I devote my time to. Brian has shown me a path to leaving a socially important legacy.

Sarah Sheard
Pittsburgh, PA, 2020

Prologue

We hope this book will help all concerned to deepen our understanding of systems engineering (SE) and better prepare us for future SE endeavors. Here we to illuminate various kinds of complex systems (CSs) and suggest learning methods that better serve us in how to recognize CSs and engineer them more effectively. SE activity in System of Systems (SoS), Enterprise Systems Engineering (ESE), and Complex Systems Engineering (CSE) continues to increase. Admittedly, there is still some controversy as to how well conventional methods of SE are able to handle our most difficult CS problems and whether new ways of "systems thinking" will help. We trust that many readers will agree that the answer to the latter portion of this issue is in the affirmative, especially after perusing this book.

Chapter 1 is essentially a tutorial, where we (1) review related definitions and terminology and (2) elaborate on defined systems and give examples of CS topics and problems as a lead-in to CSE, which is more the subject of Chapter 2.

As Chapter 2 reflects, the theory of Complex Adaptive Systems Engineering (CASE) is still evolving from learning about its practice. The chapter covers more about a number of topics (including complexity, CSs, and CSE) that purport to advance understanding in this field of endeavor. A couple of artifacts for characterizing SE environments and what is being done about it are provided. CSE principles to create "mindsights" that will accelerate progress in many application domains are presented. Finally, a cogent methodology for CSE is suggested. Chapter 2's keywords include *adaptivity, case studies, CSs, complexity, emergence, enterprises, SE, SoS,* and *systemigrams.*

In Chapter 3 we assert that most profit-making companies and other enterprises could do better in devoting more resources toward solving important world problems without detracting significantly from their primary missions. Their leaders should strive to convince key stakeholders of the virtues of such actions and the associated public-relations benefits that could well lead to increased business. Leaders and managers should psychologically and materially reward their employees for volunteering their expertise and time appropriately, depending on particular humanitarian target goals. The chapter makes a case for these premises and shows how CASE and leadership and management principles can enable progress within various CS domains exhibiting critical situations where many constituents are demanding solutions. Keywords here include *change management, CSE, moral leadership, resource allocation,* and *world problems.*

Author

Brian E. White earned an MS and a PhD in computer science at the University of Wisconsin, and SM and SB degrees in electrical engineering at the Massachusetts Institute of Technology (MIT). He served in the U.S. Air Force and for 8 years was at the MIT Lincoln Laboratory. For five years Dr. White was a principal engineering manager at Signatron, Inc. In his 28 years at The MITRE Corporation, he held a variety of senior professional staff and project/resource management positions. He was Director of MITRE's Systems Engineering Process Office from 2003 to 2009. Dr. White retired from MITRE in July 2010 and has since offered a consulting service, CAUSES ("Complexity Are Us"—Systems Engineering Strategies). He has taught technical courses as an Adjunct Professor at several U.S. universities, and he is currently tutoring in basic mathematics, calculus, electrical engineering, and complex systems. He has edited and authored several books and book chapters, mostly in his Complex and Enterprise Systems Engineering Series with Taylor & Francis and CRC Press. He has presented a dozen tutorials in complex systems and published over a hundred conference papers and journal articles in complex systems, systems engineering, digital communications, etc., over his 55+-year career.

Introduction — A Tutorial of Sorts

1

"The single best payoff in terms of project success comes from having good project definition early."

> — *RAND Corporation (Virginia A. Greiman,*
> *Megaproject Management–Lessons on Risk and Project Management from*
> *the Big Dig. Project Management Institute. Hoboken,*
> *NJ: John Wiley & Sons, Inc. 2013, p. 152)*

"It is the set of the sails, not the direction of the wind, that determines which way we will go."

> — *Entrepreneur Jim Rohm,*
> *quoted in the New Philadelphia, Ohio,*
> *Times Reporter (The Week, 1 February 2019, p. 17)*

"Some problems are so complex that you have to be highly intelligent and well informed just to be undecided about them."

> — *Educator Laurence J. Peter,*
> *quoted in the Associated Press (The Week, 4 October 2019, p. 23)*

INTRODUCTION

Much of the material provided below is taken from researching complex systems (CSs) literature and topics. This author began his quest in this field in the 2003–4 timeframe while an employee at The MITRE Corporation in Bedford, Massachusetts, United States. The "hot topics" at the time were enterprises and enterprise systems engineering (ESE). System of Systems

(SoS) generally became the more prevalent topic later, but both types of systems and the "engineering" of same were generally considered as subsets of CSs and CS engineering (CSE), respectively.

We start with definitions, a crucial area aimed at helping readers understand better what is being discussed. It's not important to agree on definitions, necessarily, but at least one can ascertain what people mean by their terminology.

Next, we elaborate on the defined systems and the notions associated with them. Much of this material is taken from courses or tutorial/workshops taught/facilitated by the author, most recently as an Adjunct Professor at the Worcester Polytechnic Institute (WPI) in Worcester, Massachusetts.

Then we get into some very important topics concerning CSs and begin to introduce CSE, primarily as a lead-in to Chapter 2.

We recommend that most readers would best be advised to only scan this chapter for portions of greater interest, depending on one's background and preparedness, and reserve more time, perhaps, for reading the main Chapters 2 and 3.

DEFINITIONS

The purpose here is to offer relatively concise definitions to the interested reader. We developed many of these definitions circa 2005 while considering a wealth of other related definitions of terms coming from credible sources. The idea is to provide one place that offers definitions upon which many individuals might reach consensus while supplying additional viewpoints for further exploration.

What's in a word? Terminology is crucial to understanding what, e.g., "enterprise systems engineering" and related words mean. Often many different terms are in use to define approximately the same entity.

Preference is given to human or human-made entities or qualities, as opposed to natural entities or qualities, because in this book we are focusing more on the human experience as opposed to the purely natural. Natural entities or qualities may be included as part of but not the whole CS being discussed, however.

Concise definitions of underlined terms used in discussions of complexity, systems, and engineering are offered. A definition may be amplified with some associated *Features* as well as appended explanatory *Note(s)*. In the interest of maintaining a semblance of brevity here, additional explanations, alternative definitions, characteristics, and/or examples of the defined terms can be explored in [1].

Complexity Terms

View, complexity, order, fitness, and *emergence* are defined below. More on interpreting "view" appears in the last (CSE) subsection of this chapter.
<u>View</u>: Any (four-tuple) combination of <u>Scope</u>, <u>Granularity</u>, <u>Mindset</u> (<u>Mindsight</u> is a better term), and <u>Timeframe</u>. Each of these latter terms is defined as follows.

<u>Scope</u>: What is included in an individual's conceptualization. *Notes*: Conceptualization is akin to perception (e.g., visualization). Specific analogies of scope are the field of view (FoV) of a camera, or more appropriately here, the "mind's eye." When one sets or determines scope, by definition, this means that everything else, not in scope, is "abstracted out," e.g., not "seen" by that individual, at least in that view, because those things are not relevant to the person's intended present state of being, e.g., purpose.

<u>Granularity</u>: The ability of a person to discern and discriminate individual items of a conceptualization.
Notes: Granularity is akin to a capability to observe details, e.g., it's like resolution. Subsets of detailed items will likely include arrangements or patterns, some of which may not be discernible in other views.

<u>Mindsight</u> (better than <u>mindset</u>): What currently captures an individual's attention in a conceptualization. *Note*: Mindsight (mindset) is akin to one's cognitive focus that may observe or contemplate, e.g., within his/her scope and with the associated granularity, a single object, pattern, notion, or idea, or collection of such elements.

<u>Timeframe</u>: The time interval of an individual's conceptualization. *Note*: Timeframe is akin to temporal component of one's conceptualization, e.g., the timescale over which it occurs.
Features: A change in any one of these elements will result in a change of view, i.e., what one can perceive/understand.
Notes: The limitations of the human brain make it practically impossible for a person to essentially grasp the underlying "reality" of any situation. Rather, each person viewing something focuses his or her mind on a mental snapshot or perspective of a situation. One understands it only to a certain extent (or scope) with its associated level of granularity (detail), abstracting out what appears to be irrelevant for one's own particular viewpoint. Even someone totally unfamiliar with ESE, for instance, can identify with the saying "If you can't change the situation, change your attitude." Attempting to take a fresh look at something familiar (mindsight) from unfamiliar points of view can be a useful device to gain further understanding of a system, perhaps in conjunction with elapsed time (timeframe).

Complexity: A technical term qualitatively describing the ultimate richness of an entity that (1) continuously evolves dynamically by organizing its own internal relationships and interacting with its environment; (2) requires multi-view analysis to perceive different non-repeating patterns of its behavior; and (3) defies methods of pre-specification, prediction, and control.

> *Features*: Complex entities possess attributes that cause them to evolve naturally without outside intervention. It is also not possible to pre-specify or predict completely and accurately what will happen with complex entities, even when one intervenes from the outside (or especially from within as an autonomous agent) with a specific purpose. The attribute of complexity is usually associated with the property of instability. Furthermore, it isn't possible to replicate complexity exactly. Each instance of a complex entity is unique. Increasing a system's complexity implies its potential behavior will display more variety, nuance, and depth. A system can become so complex that its state approaches that of chaos — and may even transition into chaos — making its nature even more difficult to understand. A system might also evolve with diminishing complexity, trending toward stability. This trend may continue to the point that the system approaches stasis — and may even transition into stasis — where it might be described as deficient in variety and richness, uninteresting, possibly stagnant, or even boring. Here stasis means rigid, inflexible, unchanging, etc. The challenge of CSE is to attempt to shape the environment of a CS by continually introducing variety and selection, akin to Ashby's "Law of Requisite Variety" [2]. This enables a system to become even more complex yet avoid chaos or stasis.
>
> *Notes*: Many people use the term "complex" as a synonym for anything that is complicated and difficult for a typical human being to understand. Although this is often appropriate in the English vernacular, when used in the context of ESE, for instance, the term "complexity" implies discerning the matter being considered in much greater depth. Like SE, complexity can be thought of as a continuum, with "complicated" at the least complex end of the scale.

Order: A qualitative measure of the instantaneous nature and extent of all specific internal relationships of an entity.

> *Notes*: Order characterizes the magnitude of the number of relationships within an entity that exist concurrently. If something has only a few relationships, it has a small order. As the number of such relationships, and the ways in which those relationships can be expressed, grow, the order increases. Order is dynamic in form and function and almost always associated with organization and things leading to that organization. Here, relationships can be thought of as patterns (among the parts of the entity) of attributes defined by values. A relationship allows the inference or deduction of the specific values of an attribute of a portion of that relationship to be based on

other attribute values of the relationship or other relationships of the entity because all those attribute values form a pattern collectively.

Fitness: The orthogonal combination of complexity and order.

> *Notes*: In the common vernacular, human fitness is the condition of being physically and mentally healthy, a quality of being suitable to fulfill a particular role or task. More generally, in biology, fitness conveys the ability to survive and reproduce in a particular environment. Both aspects of fitness (order: what currently *is*; complexity: what *could be*) are a part of how one perceives an entity.

Emergence: Something *unexpected* in the collective behavior of an entity within its environment, not clearly attributable to any subset of its parts, that is present (and observed) in a given view and not present (or observed) in any other view.

> *Notes*: Some people employ a broader definition of emergence where things that emerge can be expected as well as unexpected. We prefer to consider expected things to be intentional, designed-in, known in advance, or at least not very surprising and not warranting recognition of having an emergent property. This is done primarily to emphasize the need for a very adaptable and robust management process in the SE of CSs. It is understood that this collective behavior is in response to an entity's environment as well as the internal relationships of the entity's parts. Emergence can have benefits, consequences, or other (e.g., don't care or as yet undetermined) effects.

System Terms

Next, various terms involving the word "system" are offered.

System: An interacting mix of elements forming an intended whole greater than the sum of its parts.

> *Features*: These elements may include people, cultures, organizations, policies, services, techniques, technologies, information/data, facilities, products, procedures, processes, and other human-made or natural entities. The whole is sufficiently cohesive to have an identity distinct from its environment.
>
> *Notes*: In general, a system does not necessarily have to be fully understood, have a defined goal/objective, or have to be designed or orchestrated to perform an activity. However, in this definition, "intended" means an understood/defined goal/objective and designed/orchestrated to perform a useful activity.

System of Systems (SoS): A collection of systems that functions to achieve a purpose not generally achievable by the individual systems acting independently.

Features: Each system can operate independently (in the same environment as the SoS) and is managed primarily to accomplish its own separate purpose. An SoS can be geographically distributed and can exhibit evolutionary development and/or emergent behavior. Note: The next four definitions are from [77].

Directed SoS: The integrated SoS is built and managed to fulfill specific purposes. It is centrally managed during long-term operation to continue to fulfill those purposes as well as any new ones the system owners might wish to address. The component systems maintain an ability to operate independently, but their normal operational mode is subordinated to the central managed purpose. The collection of some systems within a modern motor vehicle can be considered an example of a Directed SoS.

Acknowledged SoS: This SoS has recognized objectives, a designated manager, and resources for the SoS; however, the constituent systems retain their independent ownership, objectives, and funding as well as development and sustainment approaches. Changes in the systems are based on collaboration between the SoS and each member system. Many components of the US air traffic management/control system can be viewed as an example Acknowledged SoS, where the Federal Aviation Administration (FAA) is the designated manager.

Collaborative SoS: In these SoSs, the component systems interact more or less voluntarily to fulfill agreed-upon central purposes. The central players collectively decide how to provide or deny service, thereby providing some means of enforcing and maintaining standards. The Internet is an example of a Collaborative SoS. The Internet Engineering Task Force (IETF) works on standards but has no power to enforce them.

Virtual SoS: These SoSs lack either a central management authority or a centrally agreed-up on purpose for the SoS. Large-scale behavior emerges — and may be desirable — but this type of SoS must rely upon relatively invisible mechanisms to maintain it. Widespread terrorism of many varieties is an example of a Virtual SoS.

Mega-System: A large, human-made, richly interconnected, and increasingly interdependent SoS.

Complex System (CS): An open system with continually cooperating and competing elements.

Features: This type system continually evolves and changes its behavior (often in unexpected ways) according to its own condition and its external environment. Changes between states of order and chaotic flux are possible.

Relationships among its elements are imperfectly known and are difficult to describe, understand, predict, manage, control, design, and/or change.

Notes: Here "open" means free, unobstructed by artificial means, and with unlimited participation by autonomous agents and interactions with the system's environment. A CS is not necessarily an enterprise (see below).

Complex Adaptive System (CAS): Identical to a complex system.

Note: Some technical people define a CAS in terms of a system, not a CS.

Homeostasis: A property of a complex system that exhibits relatively stable equilibria or behaviors among its interdependent component systems and environment.

Note: An agreed-to mission of an enterprise (see just below), like the US Department of Defense's penchant to protect our country; the Ford Motor Company's Job One, when that signified its first new car off the assembly line; and human body temperature are all examples of homeostasis.

Enterprise: A complex system in a shared human endeavor that can exhibit relatively stable equilibria or behaviors (homeostasis) among many inter-dependent component systems.

Features: An enterprise may be embedded in a more inclusive CS. External dependencies may impose environmental, political, legal, operational, economic, legacy, technical, and other constraints.
Notes: An enterprise usually includes an agreed-to or defined scope/mission and/or set of goals/objectives. Note also that this definition is meant to be limited in its complexity compared to a very complex system, for example.

As shown in Figure 1.1, the various systems defined above can be viewed as "nested" with two possible hierarchies. The enterprise is shown supreme in Figure 1.1a, whereas the complex system is superior in Figure 1.1b.

Notwithstanding the rather intricate set of definitions provided above, these two figures could be redrawn to indicate more general overlaps among the system entities. However, we prefer the nested points of view as more cogent.

Furthermore, some systems, like the solar system, may not be considered an SoS since that type of system is not managed, at least by human beings. Similarly, an SoS that is unusually dynamic may never reach a state of relative stability or become static, like the homeostasis property of an enterprise, in which case such an SoS would not be considered an enterprise. Finally, one might consider a particular kind of enterprise, say, one involving

(a)

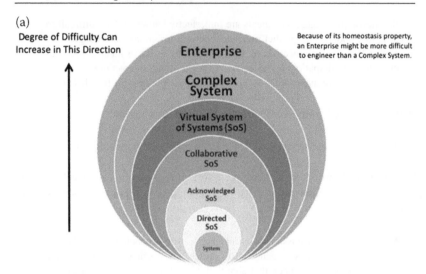

Degree of Difficulty Can Increase in This Direction

Because of its homeostasis property, an Enterprise might be more difficult to engineer than a Complex System.

(b)

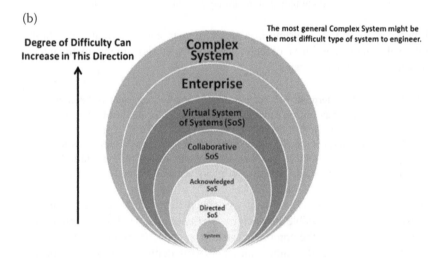

Degree of Difficulty Can Increase in This Direction

The most general Complex System might be the most difficult type of system to engineer.

FIGURE 1.1 Perceived Venn Diagram Relationships Among Systems. (a) An Enterprise is Viewed as the Most Complex. (b) A Complex System is Viewed as the Most Complex.

environmental protection driven primarily by government agencies, to be closed. In this case, the enterprise would not be a complex system.

Such nuances are quite possible depending on where one draws the system boundary. Other multifarious system examples are provided in Chapter 2.

Henceforth, we choose Figure 1.1b to serve the purpose of highlighting essential differences among these types of systems. SoSs contain systems, enterprises contain SoSs, and CSs contain enterprises. But a CS is not necessarily an enterprise, an enterprise is not necessarily a SoS, and a SoS is not necessarily a system, considering their definitions in the narrowest senses.

Engineering Terms

Next, various terms involving the word "engineering" are offered.

Engineering: Methodically conceiving and implementing viable solutions to existing problems.

> *Note*: This definition does not imply that the problems are always solved.

Enterprise Engineering: Application of engineering efforts to an enterprise with emphasis on enhancing capabilities of the whole while attempting to better understand the relationships and interactive effects among the components of the enterprise and with its environment.

> *Note*: This definition does not necessarily imply that the "best" efforts are applied. (See ESE below.)

Systems Engineering (SE): An iterative and interdisciplinary leadership, management, and development process that defines and transforms needs or "requirements" into an operational system.

> *Features*: Typically, this process involves environmental, economic, political, social, and other non-technological aspects. Activities include conceiving, researching, architecting, utilizing, designing, developing, fabricating, producing, integrating, testing, deploying, operating, sustaining, and retiring system elements.
> *Notes*: The customer for or user of the system usually states the initial version of the requirements, although these may not yet be that well understood. SE is used, in part, to help better define and refine these requirements. The so-called requirements often change as further decisions and progress are made. Hence, for conciseness, the use of the single word "defines." This definition does not imply that a successful system is always realized. And the word "integrated" is not included in this definition because systems engineering efforts may not be that well integrated.

Traditional Systems Engineering (TSE): Systems engineering but with limited attention to the non-technological and/or complex system aspects of the system.

Features: In TSE there is emphasis on the process of selecting and synthesizing the application of the appropriate scientific and technical knowledge in order to translate system requirements into a system design. Here, it is normally assumed and assured that the behavior of the system is completely predictable. Traditional engineering (not just TSE) is typically directed at the removal of unwanted possibilities.

Note: Here, it is assumed that TSE is identical to "classical" (or traditional) SE, i.e., customary and accepted methods of doing SE.

Enterprise Systems Engineering (ESE): A regimen for engineering "successful" enterprises.

Features: ESE is SE that emphasizes a body of knowledge, and tenets, principles, and precepts, having to do with the analysis, design, implementation, operation, performance, etc., of an enterprise. Rather than focusing on parts of the enterprise, the enterprise systems engineer concentrates on the enterprise as a whole and how its design, as applied, interacts with its environment. Thus, ESE avoids some potentially detrimental aspects of TSE, such as concentrating on the parts of the system and their behavior in isolation rather than how the parts interact within the system and with its outside environment in the ESE approach.

Notes: Here "regimen" means a prescribed course of engineering for the promotion of enterprise success.

Complex Systems Engineering (CSE): ESE that includes additional conscious attempts to further open an enterprise to create a less stable equilibrium among its interdependent component systems.

Features: In CSE, critical attention is paid to emergence, which can be desirable or undesirable, especially because of this penchant to expand the openness of the CS. Thus, it is important to attempt the deliberate and accelerated management of the natural processes that shape the development of CSs.

ELABORATIONS ON SOME DEFINED SYSTEMS AND THEIR NUANCES

Since one of the more popular SE topics in recent years is the treatment of SoSs, we include an expanded discussion of this type of CS next. After that, we will discuss enterprises and the most general case, CSs. Many references are provided to assist the interested readers in understanding more and/or going in further depth.

System of Systems

Here we delve into a collection of SoS topics that are worth emphasizing in providing a little more in-depth information. Some non-technological SoS factors such as

- Philosophy
- Morality/morals
- Psychology/psychological
- Culture/cultural
- Sociology/social
- Organizational change management
- Politics/political
- Law/legal
- Environment/environmental
- Economics/economic
- Legacy
- Operations/operational

head this list because these are areas that should continually be kept in mind when dealing with SoS problems in trying to apply system of systems engineering (SoSE). Something more will be said about these shortly.

- Similarly, before embarking upon SoSE, one should address *SoS leadership and management.*
- *SoS interoperability* is also important because the component systems in the SoS should be able to interoperate among themselves, not only for the benefit of the subject SoS but also that SoS's ability to interoperate with other SoSs.
- *SoS architecting* is an especially important topic because as yet there are not that many viable and agreed-to SoS architectures in existence.
- Finally, *SoS modeling and simulation* is *a propos*. One question of interest is the extent to which traditional modeling/simulation techniques can be applied to SoSs.

Non-Technological SoS Factors

One may ask why *philosophy* is on the list of non-technological factors. A thorough reading of the wonderful book on systems thinking by John Boardman and Brian Sauser [3] will likely convince most theorists and practitioners of SoSE that a broad philosophical approach is quite appropriate for better understanding SoSs and making significant progress in establishing a stronger SoSE state-of-the-art.

A discussion of *morality and the morals* one might adopt is rarely found in classical, conventional, or traditional SE. Considering the great difficulties faced by humanity's most difficult problems (cf., Chapter 3) and the far-reaching implications of SoSs in comparison with individual systems, morality rises closer to the surface as a significant motivator to do the right things as opposed to merely build things right.

Psychology is also in the forefront because people are inherently and directly involved in SoSs.

Cultures are important because people, with their diverse personal backgrounds, are motivated by their ethnicity, childhood upbringing, real-world surroundings, and adult experiences in both their careers and personal lives.

Sociology is relevant to the collective interactions of people as part of complex SoSs.

All the "soft" SE [4] methodology areas influence *organizational change management* (mainly of people) in SoS environments.

Who would deny that *politics* is relevant in an SoS development or improvement? It is not just about technology; unless the systems' stakeholders are reasonably aligned, the SoS is not going anywhere.

Many practical issues that can make or break SoS success are *legal* in nature; one cannot or should not often get away with breaking the law in developing or improving an SoS. Furthermore, *laws* may need to be modified or even created, and this also requires good politics to enable the enactors.

SoSs must often abide by *environmental* constraints, especially when they are imposed by law. In addition, *morality* and the "tragedy the commons" [5] applies here; the selfish use of an abundant common resource can be abused to the extent it declines or disappears.

Because SoSs involve multiple systems, they tend to be more expensive, particularly because of emergent properties and often because of sheer size. Thus, one needs to be as *economical* as possible in the development or improvement of an SoS.

As in classical, conventional, or traditional SE, *technology* is very important in SoSs, perhaps even more so, although all the other *technical* disciplines, particularly in the "soft" methodology areas, cannot be forgotten.

Usually SoSs are rather new initiatives, although as SoSE matures in addressing SoSs, one can conceive of more *legacy* SoSs in the future.

Finally, the *operational* fielding, maintenance, and ultimate retirement of SoSs are of interest.

SoS Leadership and Management

Leadership and management are complementary, and both are required in any form of SE.

There can be no leaders without followers. Anyone can assume the role of leader at any time, especially in situations where he or she can offer creative suggestions and innovation.

In complex environments, and in most SoS cases where SoSE is being applied, leadership is arguably more important than management. In such situations, the primary job of the leader is to create conditions for self-organization and to find ways to create incentives for and reward interactive coordination, both competition and collaboration, among the participants.

A good leader does the right things (a good manager does things right) and does not necessarily need to exude charisma, but he or she must have the ability to inspire, motivate, and command respect from followers. The leader also needs to help create a compelling vision that can easily be internalized by everyone involved in the organization's mission.

An SoS leader must be able to garner support from the leaders and managers of the component systems in the SoS, as well as his/her fellow managers of the SoS.

SoS Engineering

Here are some auxiliary thoughts about this topic.

As with CSE and ESE, neither a generally accepted theory nor a regimen for SoSE has yet been well established. Indeed, the emphasis is on trying to discover good practices in SoSE mainly through experience and best efforts but also, quite importantly, through the case studies that illuminate what works and what does not.

The principal overall challenge of SoS is to somehow motivate the proponents of each component system to increase the importance of the SoS in their minds relative to the importance of their own system. Presently this is very difficult to do because the incentive structure within each system tends to favor that system over the SoS. It is up to higher authorities in the form of governing bodies for the SoS and various component systems to ensure that adequate incentives supporting the SoS are put in place. This motivation cannot be done just by unfunded mandates from above as is often attempted in SoSs (as well as individual systems) in present practice.

Considering the four types SoSs covered in the definitions above, it logically follows that the motivation challenge increases in difficulty as one progresses from a Directed SoS to an Acknowledged, Collaborative, or Virtual SoS because there is less and less control at the SoS level over the component systems in this progression.

Perhaps the greatest success factor in an SoS development or upgrade is the extent to which the proponents of the component systems and the SoS collaborate to achieve desired SoS capabilities and interoperability among component systems. More is said about SoS interoperability below.

Collaboration will not occur automatically. As already noted, there must be appropriate incentive structures in place. From a contractual point of view, there must be flexibility to accommodate both SoS goals and the subsidiary, albeit important (from each system's point of view), goals of the component systems. One suggestion is to try to ensure that system contracts are written to give the SoS its due, e.g., by providing rewards (financial inducements, future contract advantages, etc.) when a component system satisfies an SoS goal(s). SoS authorities need to be able to replace an underperforming component system with another more capable system.

Another suggestion is to incentivize component systems to work together to share their fundamental unique values (FUVs) [6] through experimenting with laboratory or field "mash-ups." This would likely not only enhance component system interoperability but also increase SoS capabilities. Incentives for this could take several forms, viz., financial, facility access, personnel assistance, etc.

An underlying objective of all this collaboration could be the generation of systemic heuristics (rules of thumb) that might improve the decisions that those in authority, either within the component systems or the SoS, must make. It would probably be worthwhile for the SoS to staff and/or fund training as to how teams might systematically generate such heuristics.

Eberhardt Rechtin talked about stable intermediate forms within a CS (e.g., SoS) architectural framework [7, p. 91]; there will be more later about SoS architectures. Sustained periods of stability are not a characteristic of "healthy" CSs for they continually evolve as they become more robust and perhaps even "anti-fragile" [8]. On the other hand, SoSs can have at least temporary periods of relative stability. In fact, this is a good thing in terms of SoSE because of the high degree of uncertainty associated with a typical SoS's development.

A simple example by way of illustration is the construction of a parking garage in a populated area. In this endeavor, it is wise to build a very strong foundation so that floors can be added with increasing demands should the need arise. Another famous example is a George Washington Bridge spanning the Hudson River between New Jersey and New York City. Someone had the foresight to build a very strong bridge so that a second layer could be added many years later; together, they provide one-way traffic in each direction.

There are many examples where the overall goal of an SoS was too ambitious, whereas the project failed because there had been little or no planning for intermediate stages that would solidify progress in establishing a sound platform for future growth. One famous example of this was the Iridium satellite communication system, which was to provide worldwide access for voice communication. Unfortunately, the market for this did not develop because of the innovation and explosive growth of cellular mobile phones in populated areas [9].

At MIT's Engineering Systems Division (ESD), the subject of stable intermediate forms is referred to mainly as "real options," a term borrowed from the financial world of speculation but with a richer meaning in the SoSE sense. For more information refer to PhD dissertations on the topic, e.g., [10].

Rechtin also discussed something he called policy triage, a heuristic method for guiding the selection and support of SoS components [7, p. 83].

Closely related topics include innovations of extending the Design Structure Matrix (DSM) to an Engineering Systems Matrix (ESM) of much greater utility for SoSE [11] and a much more effective use of trade-space investigations, viz., [12].

Many other MIT ESD PhD dissertations relevant to SoSE can be found at https://esd.mit.edu/people/dissertations.html.

SoS Interoperability

SoS interoperability is a rather strange and limited topic. One would think that interoperability would be essentially automatic in an SoS. Further, there would be little to add in a discussion about SoS interoperability. However, this is not really the case, as will be argued here.

In most definitions (see above) an SoS is composed of a collection of systems that (1) are developed for their own purposes; (2) are generally funded and managed independently from the SoS; and (3) can continue to operate in the SoS environment even if the systems are separated from the SoS. Presumably the SoS achieves some capabilities from the interactions and the contributions of the component systems that are not already present in any subset of these systems. Those that care primarily about the SoS usually are not overly concerned about whether component systems can interoperate.

Nevertheless, if one is interested in focusing on the interoperability characteristics among the systems in the SoS, one can advocate several useful principles (that follow in *italics*) that might be kept in mind when developing systems or in aggregating systems to form an SoS.

* *Pay significant attention to horizontal integration* (as well as the more usual vertical integration) of every system. Here, improved horizontal integration means a greater likelihood that a given system will be able to interoperate successfully with other systems. This will also help in the interoperability of the SoS with other SoSs.

* *Utilize a layered architecture* in developing each system. Here, layering implies that each layer (except the topmost layer and the bottommost layer) can only interact directly with an adjacent layer. Further, the interfaces between the layers are kept as simple as possible. This has two principal advantages: (1) the system design is much "cleaner" in that the paths of influence are essentially linear instead of networked or, worse, convoluted or *ad hoc*, and (2) the implementation within a layer is free to change with better ideas or improved technology provided the interfaces between layers remain unchanged, without changing the overall behavior of the system.

* From the network perspective, *a given layer in one system can interact*, at least virtually or logically, *with the corresponding layer in any of the other systems* in a very straightforward fashion. The primary example of this is the layered communication architecture prevalent in the Internet.

* If one considers the systems of an SoS to be the network, then for enhanced interoperability, each system design team should *concentrate on the* (perhaps relatively few common) *capabilities that all systems are trying to achieve* in terms of interacting successfully with other systems of the SoS.

* Suppose there are n systems in the SoS. Unless n is very small, *one should not be overly concerned with just how one system interacts with the other* n − 1 *systems*. For example, if each system design team tries to establish the need lines or information exchange requirements between their system and all the other systems, one is facing a so-called n-squared problem, i.e., there are n(n − 1) exchanges to define; this could be a very large number unless n is very small and can be quite intractable, especially if these exchanges need to be updated periodically.

* It is much better if every team expends an effort to *make its contribution available to any other system*, without regard to knowing anything else about the other systems. Similarly, that same team

should expend an effort to *extract information of interest coming from other systems* without knowing the identity explicitly. This means the total effort expended by all the system design teams is only proportional to n, not n squared.

- Each system design team should *determine the* "fundamental unique value" (FUV) [6] of their system and emphasize that as opposed to building in all kinds of "bells and whistles," which is usually done to make sure the system is vertically integrated and able to operate on its own. The latter approach simply defeats horizontal integration, the purpose of interoperability. Rather *make each system's FUV available as a capability for other systems* that could benefit.

- Next, the system design team should *collaborate and experiment with "mash ups" of their fundamental unique values* to be assured that these values can be shared among other systems through their interactions. Clearly this will take some significant effort expenditure and sharing of information among systems. This may seem dangerous in terms of protecting intellectual property, but if this is done carefully, much sharing of information can be accomplished while protecting the systems' "crown jewels."

- In an SoS involving legacy as well as developing new systems, it is likely that some systems are so tightly vertically integrated that they cannot interoperate very well with most of the other systems. If interoperability is truly a laudable goal, then these *"culprit" systems should be redesigned, stripped down, and/or dismantled* to the extent that better horizontal integration can be achieved.

SoS Architecting

It is importance to establish an SoS architecture early on in attempting SoSE. In delving into the many architectural frameworks that may apply to SoSs, concentrate on *establishing an actual architecture* underlying the SoS problem and refrain from giving undue attention merely to the *descriptions* of that architecture, which is the main purpose of the frameworks. Unfortunately, this distinction is not understood or recognized by many so-called systems engineers.

A good place to start in creating an SoS architecture is to read Mark Maier's classic 1998 paper, "Architecting Principles for SoSs" [13].

Several existing architectural frameworks are listed below.

- Department of Defense Architecture Framework (DoDAF)
- The Enterprise Architecture

– Enterprise Architecture Management Framework (EAMF) (Developed by Dr. Paul Carlock and Robert Fenton from [14])
– Community
http://www.eacommunity.com//

• Federal Enterprise
– Architecture (FEA)
– Architecture Framework (FEAF)
– Architecture Certification Institute
http://www.feacinstitute.org//

Each of these frameworks has its own purposes, and it is unlikely that any of them are sufficient for establishing a description of an SoS architecture. For example, DoDAF is focused on military applications. Further, it was developed mainly with individual systems in mind, not SoSs. However, the framework does show how one can keep track of interconnections among systems that may be part of an SoS.

SoS Modeling and Simulation

One of the premier ways of modeling and simulating CSs such as SoSs is to use agent-based or multi-agent-based techniques.

In essence, each entity (usually of many) in the model is considered to be an autonomous agent, so-called, because that agent follows its own set of rather simple rules while interacting with other agents. The real trick in successfully performing agent-based modeling is to establish agents' necessary and sufficient set of rules to generate effective and accurate collective behavior that reflects the real world. First one postulates a set of rules, keeping them as simple and a few as possible. As one experiments with this set of rules, a given rule is added or subtracted, one at a time, to see whether each rule makes a significant difference in the result. If that rule does have a significant effect, it is retained in the set. But if that rule appears to have no measurable impact, it is deleted.

Much can be learned from this form of modeling and simulation. Often surprising results emerge that lead to additional ideas for productive simulations.

While agent-based modeling is most often used in very CS environments, it would be worthwhile to experiment with the interaction of component systems in an SoS context, treating each system as an autonomous agent following a common set of rules.

Here's a recommended recent reference to agent-based modeling [15]. Many other references can be explored in [16].

Jay W. Forrester, now deceased but formerly of MIT, is famous, among other things, for his invention (in the middle to late 1950s) and development (with many others since then) of the field of system dynamics, a philosophical method and practical set of computer-based modeling and simulation techniques that go far in helping us make sense of our most complex real-world problems and stimulating inspirations for finding solutions.

He wrote several books, *Urban Dynamics,* which appeared in February 1969; *Industrial Dynamics*, October 1963; and *World Dynamics*, August 1979. These are no longer widely available but used copies may be obtained, e.g., on Amazon.com.

There is a wonderful lecture available where Forrester tells stories about the beginning and development of system dynamics [17]. His method and simulations showed that the popular urban policy and effect of building low-cost housing for low-income and/or unemployed residents were actually counterproductive. As he said, "Such housing used up space where jobs could be created, while drawing in people who needed jobs. Constructing low-cost housing was a powerful process for creating poverty not alleviating it." This result (an example of an emerging surprise) angered several key proponents of urban renewal. It was not until they gave Forrester a chance to explain the results in detail, over several hours, did they come around to, and become strong supporters of, this point of view.

If readers would like to experiment with system dynamics, there is open course software available from MIT online to get you started: MITOPENCOURSEWARE, "System Dynamics Self Study," http://ocw.mit.edu/courses/sloan-school-of-management/15988-system-dynamics-self-study-fall-1998-spring-1999/.

Another modeling and simulation tool of high utility is something called a "systemigram," created by John Boardman and others at the Stevens Institute of Technology. The systemigram is explained in several places, e.g., in the book on systems thinking by Boardman and Brian Sauser. Here are a couple of quotes [3, pp. 100–1].

Systemigrams are based on a complete respect of the totality of problems, believing that its richness deserves to find graphical expression, and in that graphical expression inspire further detailed grammatical exposition leading to more detailed graphical description. The existence of systemigrams as a value-adding proposition, one that will reveal the inner meanings of strategic intent and help build a greater shared understanding in a growing community of people, should force up the ante for defining strategic intent more completely, more thoroughly, more thoughtfully, and more purposefully. The two go hand in hand — excellent prose and great graphics — together supporting the translation of strategy into tactics. Systemigrams are the sine qua non of strategy bridge building.

... Next for the graphic. This is to be a network, having notes and links, flow, inputs and outputs, beginning and end. This *must* fit on a single page. Key concepts, noun phrases specifying people, organizations, groups, artifacts, and conditions will be nodes. The relationships between these notes will be verb phrases (occasionally prepositional phrases) indicating transformation, belonging, and being. Nodes must be unique. Some nodes can contain other nodes, for example, to indicate breakout of a document or an organization/product/process structure. The network must be legible so that this limits the number of nodes and links. There should be no crossover of links, improving clarity this constraint further lends itself to systemic design. Such a network tends to be of an interconnected kind for which the ratio of [links to nodes] is 1.5 or thereabouts. For a systemigram of 20 nodes, the total number of possible links is 190, whereas the actual number will be about 30. This ratio [of actual to possible links] is about 15%, which is held to be the optimum ratio of interfaces in a system relative to how many there could be.

Systemigrams can be easily created with SystemiTool, a software package that is fairly intuitive and straightforward to use, supported by some documentation and a tutorial, all made available to this author (on 14 November 2014) by Brian Sauser of the University of North Texas.

SoS Summary

Here are some additional notable quotes from [3].

> Balancing perception and deception is a notion that has never been better expounded than by C. West Churchman [18], who characterized the nature of inquiry as an endless cycle of perception and deception. ... [I]n our current state of confusion where able to perceive certain patterns and truths that lead us toward light and comfort and where we are able to remain peacefully and profitably for a while until we discover that what we saw was not correct ... and we are once again trapped in confusion, but perhaps a better state than when previously deceptive conditions held us. We inquire on and discover fresh perceptions and eventually with these new patterns and truths points frisk fresh comfort. This entire cycle is humbling, a quality that serves the community well. (p. 33)

> ... Law of parsimony states that given several explanations of a specific phenomenon, the simplest is probably the best. ... William of Ockham, a fourteenth-century English philosopher and Franciscan friar, is attributed with formulating this law, known as Ockham's razor: the simplest explanation to a problem is the best explanation. For the architect this boils

down to the maxim "entities need not be needlessly multiplied." The engineer's equivalent is KISS (Keep It Simple, Stupid!). (p. 36)

... We truly believe that to lead is to serve, that to be great is to be humble, that strength comes from meekness, and that intelligence is greater for community. (p. 61)

At the end of most chapters of [3], under the Time to Think sections, there are some great problems with which we all might wrestle during some of our freer moments.

Enterprises

Here we review and expand upon the above definitions and mentions of enterprise.

Enterprises are not necessarily confined to single organizations. Government Departments or Ministries of Defense, for example, usually composed of many organizations, are enterprises because they have homeostases, i.e., overall missions to perform that provide elements of stability everyone involved is working toward [19, Chapter 1].

You might ask yourselves, "What are some other examples of enterprises? How well do these examples fit the definition offered earlier? Why or why not?" Here's another pretty good definition of enterprise.

An enterprise consists of a purposeful combination (e.g., a network) of interdependent resources (e.g., people, processes, organizations, supporting technologies, and funding) that interact with each other to coordinate functions, share information, allocate funding, create workflows, and make decisions, etc., within their environment(s) to achieve business and operational goals through a complex web of interactions distributed in space and time [20, p. 4].

The term enterprise has also been defined by others as follows:

1. One or more organizations sharing a definite mission, goals, and objectives to offer an output such as a product or service [21].
2. An organization (or cross-organizational entity) supporting a defined business scope and mission that includes interdependent resources (people, organizations and technologies) that must coordinate their functions and share information in support of a common mission (or set of related missions) [22].

3. The term enterprise can be defined in one of two ways. The first is when the entity being considered is tightly bounded and directed by a single executive function. The second is when organizational boundaries are less well defined and where there may be multiple owners in terms of direction of the resources being employed. The common factor is that both entities exist to achieve specified outcomes [23].

4. A complex, (adaptive) socio-technical system that comprises interdependent resources of people, processes, information, and technology that must interact with each other and their environment in support of a common mission [24].

What about "extended" enterprises, cf., [19, Chapter 1].

As has already been demonstrated, "enterprise" can have varied meanings depending on the context and scope. Nevertheless, many people like to think of relatively limited enterprises, like those of organizations, and then talk about extended enterprises as enterprise-like environments in which those organizations operate.

Sometimes it is prudent to consider a broader scope than merely the "boundaries" of the organizations involved in an enterprise. In some cases, it is necessary and wise to consider the "extended enterprise" in modeling, assessment, and decision making. This could include upstream suppliers, downstream consumers, and end user organizations and perhaps even "side stream" partners and key stakeholders. The extended enterprise can be defined as

> Wider organization representing all associated entities — customers, employees, suppliers, distributors, etc., — who directly or indirectly, formally or informally, collaborate in the design, development, production, and delivery of a product (or service) to the end user [25].

An enterprise includes not only the organizations that participate in it, but also people, knowledge, and other assets such as processes, principles, policies, practices, doctrine, theories, beliefs, facilities, land, intellectual property, and so on [19, Chapter 1].

Some enterprises have no readily identifiable "organizations" in them. Some enterprises are self-organizing (i.e., not organized by an external or a higher-level mandate), in that the sentient beings in the enterprise will find for themselves some ways in which they can interact to produce greater results than can be done by these individuals alone [19, Chapter 1]. Self-organizing enterprises are often more flexible and agile than if they were organized from above [26,27].

Giachetti [24] distinguishes between enterprise and organization by saying that

> an organization is a view of the enterprise. The organization[al] view defines the structure and relationships of the organizational units, people, and other actors in an enterprise.

Using this definition, we would say that all enterprises have some type of organization, whether formal, informal, hierarchical, or self-organizing network.

From an SE point of view, you may ask why should we be concerned about enterprises as opposed to simpler systems or more complicated (or complex) SoSs? In the 2003–5 timeframe, there was a growing awareness (e.g., at The MITRE Corporation) of serious problems in applying SE techniques effectively to large systems (sometimes called mega-systems), SoSs, and enterprises [20, Foreword].

> ... [S]omething had changed in the way people worked together, both within the general population and the systems engineering discipline. Seldom did isolated groups work on local problems to build stove-piped solutions. Seldom were systems developed or used in a social, political, economic, or technical vacuum. It seemed that everyone and everything were interconnected and interdependent.

> Changes in the sociocultural and technical landscape had repercussions on the practice of systems engineering. Requirements changed faster than they could be met; risks shifted in a never-ending dynamic of actions and reactions within the network of stakeholders; configurations changed with rapidly changing technology cycles; and integrated testing was faced with trying to match the scale and complexity of the operational enterprise. Processes that managed requirements, risks, configurations, and tests, four [aspects] of [TSE], were confounded by their complex environment.

> ... What is an *enterprise*? What are its *boundaries*? What are the *scales* of the enterprise ...? How do you define *requirements*? ... [When] one [draws] the boundary of the enterprise, there [are] influences coming in from outside that boundary. [There are] multiple and seemingly incommensurate levels of the enterprise: the individual systems, groups of systems [SoSs] performing a cooperative mission, and the enterprise as a whole. Requirements [can change] routinely. ... [T]he enterprise boundary [can be] defined to include all those elements we [might] either control or influence; [there could be] three tiers — individual systems, [SoSs], and enterprise; and ... requirements [could be] defined in terms of enterprise outcome spaces

without any obvious allocation down to systems or subsystems. There [is still] no established theory to guide our choices.

An enterprise may require a particular operational capability that is brought into being by connecting together a chain of systems that together achieve that capability. Any one of these systems in the chain cannot by itself provide this capability. The desired capability is the emergent property of this chain of systems. This chain of systems is sometimes called an SoS. However, the enterprise that requires this capability rarely has direct control over all the systems necessary to provide this full capability [28]. Not only that, some portions of an enterprise may not be able to operate on its own in that enterprise's environment.

There is a general issue regarding dealing with enterprises in this situation: there are at least two enterprises related to any particular SoS. First, there is the enterprise of builders/developers comprising projects and programs, which have to be organized appropriately and adopt special types of architectural principles. Second, there is the enterprise of users (those who use the products and service provided by the first enterprise), which has to exercise its own sort of agility. How the first enterprise designs systems to allow the second to operate is the core issue.

The Enterprise as a System

To enable more efficient and effective enterprise transformation, the enterprise needs to be looked at "as a system" rather than as a collection of functions connected solely by information systems and shared facilities [29-31]. What distinguishes the design of enterprise systems from product systems is *the inclusion of people* as a featured component of the system, not merely as a user/operator of the system [32].

> The term "enterprise system" has taken on a narrow meaning of only the information system an organization uses. Research and project experience have taught us that to design a good enterprise system, we need to adopt a much broader understanding of enterprise systems. The greater view of enterprise systems is inclusive of the processes the system supports, the people who work in the system, and the information [and knowledge] content of the system [24].

It is worth noting that the concept of "service" systems also includes people in the system. The thoughts above do not take this into account, primarily since their perspectives come mainly from a product system experience. The practice of service (SE) is relatively new and is an emerging discipline.

The primary purpose of an enterprise is to create value for society (cf., Chapter 3 of this book), other stakeholders, and for the organizations that participate in that enterprise.

There are three types of organizations of interest: businesses (see Note 1 below), projects, and teams. A typical business participates in multiple enterprises through its portfolio of projects. Large SE projects can be enterprises in their own right, with participation by many different businesses, and may be organized as a number of sub-projects.

Note 1. The use of the word "business" is not intended to mean only for-profit commercial ventures. As used here, it also includes government agencies and not-for-profit organizations, as well as commercial ventures. Business is the activity of providing goods and services involving financial, commercial, and industrial aspects.

An enterprise must strive towards two main objectives: (1) develop things within the enterprise to serve as either external offerings or as internal mechanisms to enable achievement of enterprise operations and (2) transform the enterprise itself so that it can most effectively and efficiently perform its operations and survive in its competitive and constrained environment [19, Chapter 1].

COMPLEX SYSTEMS

This subsection introduces the technical notions of complexity and discusses complex problems and the importance of getting a handle on how architecture can help in dealing with CSs. Then we emphasize the relevance of a number of topics, viz., requirements, self-organization, leadership, co-evolution, opportunity and risk, and modularity.

Degrees of Complexity

Many SE practitioners tend to use the words complex and complicated interchangeably. This is unfortunate because systems that include people are always complex because people are. Challenging systems, even those that "boggle the mind" but that do not intentionally include people as part of the system, are really only complicated, or at least not as complex, compared to those that do. People are fundamentally autonomous, independent CSs [19], but their interactions are what make situations very complex. On the other hand, many people behave in ways that are not that independent and autonomous in that they are significantly influenced by their beliefs and behavior of others. Thus all this is a "gray area."

Partly in order to attain a better grasp of what CSs are about, it is worthwhile to think of specific examples and to suggest to what degree they are complex. We have chosen five categories, merely complicated and low, medium, high, and very high complexity. However, these category names, describing relative intensity, are quite inadequate in suggesting how seriously difficult all these examples are in hoping to create improved conditions or satisfactory solutions.

Here are ten systems in order of decreasing complexity, chosen "off-the-top-of-the-head" and clearly representing degrees of opinion. Very high complexity includes fighting international terrorism and reducing global climate change. High complexity means marginalizing Iran, North Korea, et al., and bolstering renewable energy. Medium complexity would involve updating government acquisition and re-building national infrastructure. Low complexity refers to fixing cyber security and innovating in social networks. Finally, merely complicated includes developing military systems and improving air traffic control.

The very high complexity category reflects essentially all of the CSs characteristics and behaviors discussed in Chapter 2. (You might want to take a temporary break here and look ahead to preview them.) Most of these apply for high complexity category, some apply in medium complexity, and a few apply in low complexity. Arguably, the merely complicated category could also include a few characteristics and behaviors unless, of course, people are included in these examples, in which case they would become more complex.

Extremely Complex Problems

The world is faced with a large number of extremely complex system problems. A few of the most pressing ones include hunger, water shortage, unlimited material growth, overpopulation, intolerance, and human migration.

There is widespread world hunger despite the existence of lots of arable land, huntable forests/plains, fishable waters, and bird-infested atmospheres. This problem is related to the low economic status of the most-needy peoples and the high cost of distributing food to the most demanding regions of the Earth.

Fresh potable water is becoming in ever shorter supply as populations expand, especially in the more underdeveloped countries of the world.

Clearly, water shortages could be a major cause of future international conflicts and wars, especially between abutting countries.

In Western nations at least, we are taught from childhood that growth is inherently good for its own sake. As "civilized" people mature, they become accustomed to competing to acquire more and more goods of a material nature. Because the Earth is a finite resource, the ever-increasing efforts to tap its riches could eventually become unsustainable [33].

The preceding three problems are exacerbated by the world's ever-increasing population. We've grown from two or three billion to more than seven billion in just over 50 years, and we will likely approach nine billion people within two or three decades [34]. Despite many technological advances and the Earth's remarkable resilience, many people are still dying because of natural disasters, wars, and terrorism. Indeed, there are limits to human sustainability. As this population trend continues worldwide, our quality of life on Earth will continually deteriorate and ultimately suffer. In this regard, it is interesting to contemplate the impacts and effects of the COVID-19 pandemic on the threats of overpopulation.

An acceptable quality of life is also hampered by widespread intolerance among peoples and nations regarding unacceptable societal norms, religious extremism, and the worship of money. These are some of the reasons why we are all unable to live together in peace and harmony. It does not help that a significant minority among the human population (perhaps as high as 4%) have no conscience and feel no guilt about taking advantage of their fellow human beings [35].

The physical migration of the downtrodden and economically disadvantaged is becoming more prevalent in recent years. United States and several European countries such as Britain, Germany, and France are undergoing increasing pressures to handle immigrants in a welcoming and humane fashion. It is ironic that whereas many Americans used to boast about how the United States was a melting pot welcoming all peoples, now cannot even muster Congressional support in attempting to revamp immigration laws. One sometimes wonders whether we might someday have to begin migrating to extraterrestrial locations, both natural and unnatural [36].

Realistically speaking, how many of us can actually expect much progress to be made on any of these vital issues concerning the future of humanity? Certainly, few of us have jobs that even remotely approach doing good for humankind. Further, career opportunities that would ensure progress are relatively scarce and unattractive. Private enterprises are mainly concerned with showing profits. Many governments are dominated by politics and various levels of corruption, so they are not expected to lead in addressing these very complex problems. Nevertheless, highly motivated individuals and small groups can make a difference. Who knows, some well-intentioned efforts might catch on and expand in helping to change the world for the better.

After all, in order to receive pay/salary and benefits, one must serve organizational goals. At least this can be done while trying to motivate and enlist one's constituents toward broader efforts that would benefit humankind. The saner among us can use conscience as a guide in such endeavors. If sufficient results are not forthcoming, the braver among us might even change organizations. More of this theme is found in Chapter 3 of this book.

Complex Architecture Considerations

While TSE projects are focused on requirements in developing a new product or service the architecture needs to emphasized.

For example, Wilber [37] illustrates the complex architecture on the Boeing 787 (cf., the case study of [19, Chapter 23]), which includes communication with the airport, the industry, the airline, private and public networks, and the general manufacturing process. This architecture includes major elements of the passenger environment, cabin and airline services, maintenance, open networking, avionics data, and the flight deck. Other elements include support of maintenance performance, airplane health management, airline flight operations and materials management through the supply chain.

Various descriptions can be used to describe architectures for CSs:

Description a

Designing the architecture of a complex SoS, cf., [19, Chapter 2], is illustrated in [38].

Description b

Architecture is particularly important for the following reasons given by [39].

1. Architecting deals largely with the unmeasurable using nonquantitative tools whereas engineering uses the hard sciences
2. The word architecting refers only to the process; architecting is an invented word to describe how architectures are created, much as engineering describes how engines and other artefacts are created
3. The history of classical architecting suggests that the process of creating architectures began in Egypt more than 4000 years ago with the pyramids

4. However, designing a modern computer program also requires architecting
5. This architecting is a response to complexity in the system and explains why a single optimum solution never exists: there are just too many variables (p. 6)
6. However, this complexity also requires a systems approach specifically linking value judgements and design decisions
7. Critical details in the architect's design will be the system's connections and interfaces; secondly will be this system components; this combination produces unique system level functions; this is because the system specialists are likely to concentrate most on the core and least on the periphery of their subsystems
8. Modelling is the creation of abstractions or representations of the system in order to predict and analyse performance, costs, schedules, and risks and to provide guidelines for systems research, development, design, manufacture, and management (p. 12)
9. Architecting is the embodiment of project strategy

Description c

Crawley et al. [40] make the following points. Architecture

1. is an abstract description of the entities of the system and interconnections and interaction
2. is the link between form and function
3. provides rules to follow when creating a system
4. is important because it provides guidance and structure to later phases of system design
5. provides handles for addressing
    a. alternative form
    b. substructure and modules
    c. complexity
    d. flexibility
    e. other "ilities"
6. invites abstract thinking about unifying themes based on structure and arrangements
7. is used to:
    a. Define and manage interfaces
    b. Standardise components
    c. Standardise interfaces
    d. Systematise integration, verification and validation of the lower levels

Description d

Dahmann (who focuses exclusively on SoSs, not the more general enterprises or complex systems) addresses [41] the following areas.

1. Translating SoS capability objectives into high-level requirements over time
2. Understanding the components of the SoS and their relationships over time
3. Assessing the extent to which the SoS meets capability objectives of the time; developing, evolving, and maintaining a design for the SoS
4. Monitoring and assessing potential impacts of changes on SoS performance
5. Addressing the requirements on SoS and solution options
6. Orchestrating upgrades to the SoS

Description e

Gharajedaghi [42, pp. 152–184] proposes the following approach to designing business architecture.

1. Identifying the system's boundaries and business environment
2. Developing the system's purpose
   a. This is not always obvious because "emerging consequences contradict expectations because the operating principles are rooted in assumptions that belong to different paradigms."
   b. The basic business model is relevant here as this defines how the business generates value, creates a deliverable package and exchanges it for money or other forms of reward.
3. Identifying functions
   a. Selecting a product/market niche is important here and competitive advantage has to be considered.
4. Identifying structure
   a. Traditional organisations are based on structurally defined tasks, segmentation and hierarchical coordination of functions;
   b. SoS requires more distributed leadership.
5. Outputs dimensions
   a. "... [T]he output dimensions or platform consists of a series of general purpose, semiautonomous, and ideally self-sufficient units

charged with all the activities of responsible for achieving the organisation's mission introduction of its outputs."

6. Markets dimensions
   a. This is the interface with customers.
7. Organisational or business processes
   a. Processes are required to create integration, alignment and synergy among the organisation's parts.
8. Planning, learning and control system
9. Measurement system

Description f

Dagli and Kilicay-Ergin [43] see SoS architecting as including:

1. Architecting properties
   a. abstract, meta level
   b. fuzzy uncertain requirements
   c. network centric
   d. software intensive
   e. people intensive
   f. intensive communication infrastructure
   g. networks of various stakeholders
   h. collaborative emergent development
   i. dynamic architecture

2. Architecting constraints
   a. emphasis on interface architecting to foster collaborative functions among independent systems
   b. concentration on choosing the right collection of systems to satisfy the requirements
   c. scalability
   d. interoperability
   e. trustworthiness
   f. hidden cascading failures
   g. confusing life cycle context.

3. Legacy systems
   a. abstraction level determines the integration of legacy systems to other systems
   b. balance of heuristics, analytical techniques and integration modelling.

Description g

Revolution presents challenges due to changes in the system context. Dynamic changing requirements increase uncertainty and systems need to be designed for fuzzy attributes. Key questions arise including

1. How can we assure trustworthiness?
2. How can we assure interoperability?
3. How can we reassure large-scale design along with distributed testing?
4. How can we assure evolutionary growth?
5. How can we deal with hidden interdependencies?
6. How can we guard against cascading failures?

The plug and play concept of assembling and organising coalitions from different systems provides flexibility to respond to a changing operational and environmental situation.

The information dream architecture is the backbone of the SoS architecture.

Other Questions

There are some important questions that need to be addressed about the role of architecture in complex projects. The following will attempt to gather data to address relevant issues.

1. What are the differences among the architectures...?
2. Was the vision for the project clearly expressed in the architecture?
3. Were values addressed in the architecture?
4. Were requirements addressed in the architecture?
5. Were the core and peripheral elements in the system design and structure recognised?
6. Was a DSM [11] created in developing the architecture?
7. If a DSM was developed, were design rules also developed?
8. To what extent was there an attempt to modularise the software in the system architecture: not much; a little; a lot; it was a dominant approach.

Building these issues into the architecture of SoSE initially appears to be the most secure approach. "Architecture dictates the form and function by which design decisions can be made." Azani [44] endorses the view that "there seems to be a consensus that the architecture is the structure not only of the systems, but of its functions, the environment in which it will move, and the processes by which it will be built and operated."

Khoo [45] supports this approach in commenting that the use of closed requirements to specify systems must be amended to become open and flexible; however, he comments that there lacks the express power to rigorously capture complexity. Khoo also comments that government contracting and procurement processes are too restrictive to assist this process.

Two of Maier's and Rechtin's comments need to be remembered: "Architecture is the embodiment of strategy," and one clarifies the problem as one develops the solution [39].

However, developing architectures of SoS and SoSE has been fraught with difficulty. Meilich comments that "an adaptive architecture will be required to support operations that may change on the battlefields of the future" [46]. He sees a problem in developing a template for architecture of SoS because they have to operate in changing contexts and adapt to changing mission. He finally concludes that developing architecture of SoSE is too challenging a task at this stage.

Bjelkemyr et al. [47] endorse the need for architecture of SoS because this will help define a clear purpose and apparent boundaries. They recognize that the "internal properties of SoS resemble those of an organism." However, while contributing concepts on architecture, they conclude that significantly more research is required. DeLaurentis and Crossley [48] provide a hierarchical framework for describing SoS and a taxonomy for guiding design methods. However, they conclude that "a comprehensive set of methods for design in a SoS context do not yet exist and more development effort is needed."

Given the previous discussion that there is no agreed architectural template for SoSE or CSE, it is concluded that the contributions to SoSE from CSs research need to be recognized as processes rather than embedded in architecture at this stage, as this as far as we can go at present.

Any reader interested in more recent results in the realm of CSE architectures is invited to do further literature searches and report the results.

Requirements Complexity

Sarah Sheard, in her PhD dissertation on Complexity and Systems Engineering [49], found that there were three complex aspects of early projects that correlated significantly with cost, schedule, and performance problems. These were as follows.

Requirements Difficulty

Difficult requirements are considered at least elusive to implement or engineer, are hard to trace to the sources, and have higher degrees of overlap with other requirements. If there are a number of difficult requirements, it may be questionable that a system that performs the required functions can be built at all. Higher numbers of difficult requirements typified projects that had more manageable changes in needs and more problematic stakeholder interactions.

Cognitive Fog

Cognitive fog is found primarily when the project finds itself in a mess of conflicting data and cognitive overload. On projects that developed less cognitive fog,

1. the project had [fewer] cost overruns, scheduled delays, and replanning
2. the projects started with more easy and nominal product requirements
3. there was more architectural precedence (but this was not significant)
4. there was less conflict among technical requirements and between technical requirements and cost and schedule constraints on the project
5. there were fewer changes in limbo at any given time, fewer changes in stakeholder needs during the project, and more stakeholder concurrence

Cognitive fog relates to the prior and later variables and is exacerbated by

1. A larger number of the decision makers
2. Larger amounts of stakeholder conflict and changes in stakeholder needs
3. A high degree of requirements and changes in limbo
4. Political arguments
5. Instability and conflicting data

Stable Stakeholder Relationships

Projects with stable stakeholder relationships had

1. Less replanning
2. Fewer stakeholder conflicts
3. More concurrence amongst stakeholders
4. Lower cost overruns, scheduled delays, and performance shortfalls
5. Higher subjective success
6. Less conflict among technical requirements
7. Less cognitive fog
8. Less change in stakeholder needs.

Sensitivity to Initial Conditions

The initial conditions of CSs determine where they currently are and, consequently, two CSs that initially had their various elements and dimensions very close together can end up in distinctly different places due to their nonlinear relationships ... [50, p. 27].

Phase space addresses the evolution of systems by considering the evolution process as a sequence of states in time [51]. A state is the position of the system in its phase space at a given time. At any time, the system's state can be seen as the initial conditions for whatever processes that follow. ... All interactions are contingent on what has previously occurred [50, p. 27].

"This is closely related to the notion of 'path dependence,' which is the idea that many alternatives are possible at some stages of a system's development, but once one of these alternatives gains the upper hand, it becomes 'locked in' and it is not possible to go to any of the previous available alternatives." For example,

> ... [M]any cities developed where and how they did not because of the "natural advantages" we are so quick to detect after the fact, but because their establishment set off self-reinforcing expectations and behaviours [Cronon, cited in [52] and then [50, p. 28].

Complexity, nonlinearity of behaviour, and sensitivity to initial conditions make it extremely difficult to separate the contributions to overall behaviour that individual factors have. Therefore, any notion of "good practice" requires a detailed local knowledge to understand why the practice in question was good.

It is necessary to incorporate an acceptance of the inherent levels of uncertainty into planning. ... A realistic understanding of this uncertainty is required and there is a need to build a level of flexibility and adaptability into projects to provide greater resilience ... [50, p. 30].

Self-Organization

Self-organization is a form of emergent property and supports the notion that CSs cannot be understood in terms of the sum of their parts, since they may not be understood from the properties of individual agents and how they may behave when interacting in large numbers.

Mitleton-Kelly [53, pp. 19–20] points out that self-organization, emergence, and the creation of new order are three of the key characteristics of CSs. She reminds us that Kauffman [54] focuses on Darwinian natural selection as a "single singular force" and argues that "[i]t is this single-force view which I believe to be inadequate, for it fails to notice, fails to stress, fails to incorporate the possibility that simple and complex systems exhibit order spontaneously" [54, p. xiii]. However, Pinker [55] seems to espouse the inclusion of that possibility. Spontaneous order is self-organization.

Mitleton-Kelly [53, pp. 19–20] adds that

> [E]mergent properties, qualities, patterns, or structures, arise from the interaction of individual elements; they are greater than the sum of the parts and may be difficult to predict by studying the individual elements.

Emergence is the *process* that creates new order together with self-organization. She also reminds us that Checkland defines emergent properties as those exhibited by a human activity system "as a whole entity, which derives from its component activities and their structure, but cannot be reduced to them" [4, p. 314]. The emphasis is on the *interacting whole* and the *nonreduction* of those properties to individual parts.

Self-organization may be described in an arrangement when a group spontaneously comes together to perform a task.

The concept of self-organization echoes emergent properties and the fact that a CS cannot be understood as the sum of its parts, since it may not be discernible from the properties of the individual agents and how they may behave when interacting in large numbers. For example, studies have shown how highly segregated neighborhoods can arise from only low levels of racism in individuals ... Various kinds of markets are probably exemplary examples of self-organizing systems. As the Nobel Laureate Ilya Prigogine has put it in [56], "The economy is a self-organising system, in which market structures are spontaneously organised by such things as the demand for labour and demand for goods and services."

Westley et al. [57] argue that

> Bottom-up behaviour [leading to self-organisation] seems illogical to Western minds ... we have a hierarchical bias against self-organisation ...

[which is displayed in our common understanding of how human change happens, especially in organisations]. Our popular management magazines are filled with stories of the omniscient CEO [Chief Executive Officer] or leader who can see the opportunities or threats in the environment and leads the people into the light. *However*, self-organisation is critical to achieving *change*.

Ramalingam et al. [50] point out that self-organization describes how the adaptive strategies of individual agents in particular settings are able to give rise to a whole range of emergent phenomena, including the emergence of resilience (pp. 49–50). They further note that self-organization need not necessarily be about change as it can be about resilience in the face of change. They see resilience being about continuous and often simultaneous stages of release, reorganization, exploitation, and conservation, including the possibility of destruction of some existing organizational structures. This frees up essential resources and enables growth in new areas. Cycles of destruction in economies release innovation and creativity. Reorganization is where there is competition for available resources, which are then exploited by the dominant species or winning proposal.

Leadership (also, see [24] from Chapter 3)

The role of leadership is important in terms of self-organization of complex systems. Marion and Uhl-Bien [58] suggest that in CSs there is a need for different leadership qualities. Ramalingam et al. [50] point out that the traditional perspective of leadership (*in Western society?*) is based on a view of organizations as mechanical systems [59], [60]. This is made up of highly prescriptive rule sets, formalized control, and hierarchical authority structures. Leaders are expected to contribute to stabilisation through directive actions, based on planning for the future and controlling the organizational response. However, in CSs, the future cannot be predicted, and change cannot be directed.

Leaders of self-organised adaptive agents are characterised by their ability to (1) disrupt existing patterns by creating and highlighting conflicts, (2) encourage novelty, and (3) use "sense making." Each of these is worth exploring in a little more detail, cf., Plowman et al. [61], [62], cited by Ramalingam et al. [50, p. 51]. Leaders disrupt existing patterns by acknowledging and embracing uncertainty, refusing to back away from uncomfortable truths, talking openly about the most serious issues, and challenging institutional "taboos," which encourage more open thinking about the new ideas and patterns to emerge. An effective method for communicating in this way is provided by Knowles [63].

Uhl-Bien et al. [64] developed the concept of complexity leadership that is quite different from traditional command and control leadership and is suitable to fast-paced volatile contracts in the knowledge era. Complexity leadership uses the concept of complex adaptive systems (CAS) and "recognises that leadership should not be seen only as position and authority but also as an emergent, interactive dynamic — a complex interplay from which a collective impetus for action and change emerges when heterogeneous agents interact in networks in ways that produce new of behaviour or new modes of operating." For the purposes of this chapter, the question is the extent to which complexity leadership applies in SoS projects.

Uhl-Bien et al. [64] propose a leadership framework they call Complexity Leadership Theory (CLT). Within CLT they recognize three broad types of leadership: (1) leadership grounded in traditional bureaucratic notions of hierarchy, alignment, and control, which they call administrative leadership; (2) leadership that structures and enables conditions such as CAS and is able to optimally address creative problem solving, adaptability, and learning; and (3) leadership as a generative dynamic that underlies emergent change activities, which they call adaptive leadership.

Complexity leadership is embedded in context, which is the "ambiance that spawns a given systems dynamic personae." This CSs persona refers to the nature of interactions and interdependencies among agents (people and ideas), hierarchical divisions, organizations, and environments. CAS and leadership are socially constructed in and from this context. The theory distinguishes between leadership and leaders in which leadership is an emergent, interactive dynamic that is produced out of adaptive outcomes. This theory recognises that leadership theory has largely focused on leaders, their actions as individuals, and seeing leadership as a dynamic systems concept and processes that comprise leadership. Complexity leadership occurs in the face of adaptive challenges that are typical of the knowledge era rather than technical problems or characteristic(s) of the industrial age.

Our McCarter and White book [65] contains additional reference material relevant to complex[ity] leadership.

A fresh look at leadership recognising that it is embedded in context and goes beyond the notion of individual leaders to recognise leadership processes. Complexity leadership recognises the difference between complicated and complex organizations, in which a jumbo jet is complicated, but a rainforest is complex [66]. Complexity leadership is intensely adaptive and innovative [66,67], which is assisted by being loosely coupled. Coupling imposes restrictions on adaptation [54,67] and bottom-up behavior has more opportunity to succeed. Informal emergence can occur if internal controls do not hinder demands imposed by environmental exigencies. Such constraints are valuable for allocating resources, controlling costs, and coordinating action.

CASs are unique and desirable in their ability to adapt rapidly and creatively to environmental changes. CSs enhance their capacity for adaptive response to environmental problems or internal demand by diversifying their behaviors or strategies. Diversification, from the perspective of complexity science, is defined as increasing internal complexity (the number and level of interdependent relationships, heterogeneity of skills and outlooks within the CAS, and attention to the point of, or exceeding, that of competitors or the environment); CSs usually have the sufficient complexity referring to Ashby's requisite variety [2]. "This law simply states that the system must possess complexity equal to that of the environment in order to function effectively" [64, p. 301]. To do so, it must release the capacity of a neural network of agents in pursuit of such optimisation; that is, the system must learn and adapt. By contrast, traditional organizations have done the opposite in simplifying adaptation.

Co-Evolution

When adaptable autonomous agents or organisms interact intimately in an environment, such as in predator-prey and parasite-host relationships, they influence each other's evolution. This effect is called co-evolution, and it is the key to understanding how all large-scale CASs behave over the long term. Each adaptive agent in a CS has other agents of the same and different kinds as part of its environment. As the agent adapts to its surroundings, various elements of its surroundings are adapting to it and each other. Co-evolution is one important result of the interconnectedness of adaptive bodies. This means that "the evolution of one domain or entity is partially dependent on the evolution of other related domains or entities" [68]. A commonly cited example, elephants thrive on acacia trees, but the latter can only develop in the absence of the former. After a while, the elephants destroy the trees, drastically changing the wildlife that the area can sustain and even affecting the physical shape of the land. In the process, they render the area uncongenial to themselves, and they either die or move on.

Work in biology on "fitness landscapes" is an interesting illustration of competitive co-evolution [68]. A fitness landscape is based on the idea that the fitness of an organism is not dependent only on its intrinsic characteristics but also on its interaction with its environment. The term "landscape" comes from visualizing a geographical landscape of fitness "peaks," where each peak represents an adaptive solution to a problem of optimising certain kinds of benefits to the species. The fitness landscape is most appropriately used where there is a clear single measure of the fitness of an entity, so may not always be useful in social sciences [50, pp. 53–54].

Also refer to [69] for Richard Dawkins's profound discussion of co-evolution.

Opportunity and Risk

The importance of opportunity management should increase qualitatively as one proceeds from system, to system of systems (SoS), to enterprise views. This is partially based on the premise, supported by historical fact and *ad hoc* observations, that risk management tends to dominate at a systems view. At an enterprise view, the author has tried to develop the rationale for paying much more attention to opportunity management than risk management. It might then follow that opportunity management and risk management would be roughly co-equal at an SoS view. Nevertheless, this should be treated just notional at this point. Further testing of hypotheses concerning the greater importance of opportunity management at SoS and enterprise views is appropriate. The minimum goal of this presentation is to raise your sensitivity level to proactively pursuing opportunities at all engineering views.

Opportunity and risk can be thought of as assessable uncertainties. Clearly, there exist unassessable uncertainties and unknown uncertainties, so the topic of uncertainty management is more general that what is treated here. This beyond-present-scope idea is merely acknowledged, as there is no present attempt to depict relative magnitudes of these uncertainties.

We are operating in the domain of opportunity, principally, when developing a system concept; traditional focus on risk tends to intensify after that in terms of what can go wrong in trying to realize the system. If we implicitly assume that one is already into the development of a system, SoS, or enterprise, the greatest enterprise risk may be in not pursuing enterprise opportunities. Enterprise risk, *per se*, is mainly concerned with keeping the enterprise "healthy," i.e., open to future possibilities of change.

There is duality in treating risks and opportunities among systems, SoS, and enterprises. As the views and associated emerging patterns change from systems to enterprises, we assert that opportunities become more important.

Opportunity (as well as risk) management is a "team sport." Everyone should be sensitive to what is happening and participate in altering course, as appropriate. This becomes more challenging in enterprise environments. ESE is the "big leagues" for opportunity management.

Keep in mind there are unknowns and unknowables. One is advised to be rather humble when confronting the complexities of the enterprise.

Opportunities in ESE abound! Be open to them in creative ways while being mindful of the need to monitor results carefully to protect against stagnation or even chaos.

Qualitative assessments of opportunity management tend to be more difficult for enterprises than for SoS or systems. These assessments could easily change after learning more about ESE.

Our principal hypothesis can be summarized as the following: In ESE, be aggressive with opportunity and accept risk. This is just the opposite of what one might think of as a corresponding TSE tenet! Nevertheless, additional hypothetical examples of this and, better yet, validation from actual case studies, should be sought.

Future work could include the exploration of "Real Options to give weight to upside opportunities associated with uncertainty, in addition to the traditional concern with downside losses and risks" [70].

Modularity

Modularity is typically defined as a continuum describing the degree to which a system's components may be separated and recombined. It refers to both the tightness of coupling between components and the degree to which the "rules" of the system architecture enable (or prohibit) the mixing and matching of components. Its use, however, can vary somewhat by context. Modularity refers to the idea that a system is composed of independent, closed, domain-specific processing pieces or subsystems called modules.

Modularity makes the complexity of the system manageable by providing divisions within the system, thus enabling parallel work [71, p. 6].

When faced with a risky design process, which has a wide range of potential options, it is worthwhile experimenting with the modular breakdown. Options interact with modularity in a powerful way. By definition, a modular architecture allows modular designs to be changed and improved over time without undercutting the functionality of the system as a whole.

A layered architecture, that in addition insists that the interfaces between any two adjacent layers remain relatively simple, is generally even better than a modular architecture [72].

A series of design rules can be created by experimenting with modularity.

The design of CSs can be mapped through use of a DSM [11] that integrates the interactions between various components of the system. Thus, changes can be made to the membership of components that will support and enhance modularity.

COMPLEX SYSTEMS ENGINEERING

Here are a few additional remarks on complex systems engineering. More can be found in Chapters 2 and 3.

Interpreting Scale (or View) and Emergence in Complex Systems Engineering

A human-centric treatment of the concepts of multi-scale analysis and emergence in CSE is offered. This includes an attempt to characterize what an individual might do in conceptualizing a given SE situation s/he is facing. The goal is to suggest fresh interpretations of the terms scale and emergence that will contribute to a more collaborative approach to improving the CSE practice. Because other authors use "scale" in several different ways, potentially causing confusion, this author proposes "view" instead. Here, a given view as defined previously as a combination of "scope," "granularity," "mindset," and "timeframe." Although "emergence" has a rich spectrum of definitions in the literature, this author prefers to emphasize the unexpected, especially "surprising," flavor of emergence.

Kuras and White [73] assert that multi-scale (multi-view) analysis is crucial to the more effective CSE. It should not be unexpected that a number of carefully chosen perspectives can reveal, albeit sometimes surprising, patterns that help one better understand complex systems. These different views, together, may elicit ideas for influencing or shaping the environment of a complex system to help guide or shape it towards more useful capabilities.

Practice Drives Theory

In science, which is all about understanding the universe, very often theory drives practice. For example, based upon their objective observations, physicists first develop a theory that gains some degree of acceptance, among fellow scientists at least. This holds until the theory is proven wrong by the practice of conducting experiments.

In engineering, which is all about solving human-made problems, the reverse tends to be true, i.e., practice drives theory. First comes the concept, then the practice, and then the theory.

Suppose 1950 is taken as the year when classical, traditional, or conventional SE was invented. In this era Jay Forrester of MIT invented system dynamics [17] as we have already noted, for example. Let us assume that SE was practiced from the late 1950s through about 1990 (and beyond) when the National Council on Systems Engineering (NCOSE) (now the International Council On Systems Engineering [INCOSE]) was formed. Thus, 1990 might be is taken as the demarcation where SE theory began.

CSE is next mainly because the scientific field of complexity extends back into at least the 1940s, prior to our start date of 1950. The practice of CSE began circa 1993 with Yaneer Bar-Yam's efforts [74] in making the study of complexity more practical and actionable. Theoretical methodologies for CSE began in earnest just prior to 2006 with proposals by Doug Norman, Mike Kuras, and Brian White et al. [75,76].

Arguably, ESE began about 1958 with the formation of The MITRE Corporation. In an MITRE-officer driven effort, senior staff began a formal study of ESE theory in late 2003.

Finally, the practice of SoSE began circa 1998 with Mark Maier's definition of SoSs [13]. Significant efforts toward a theory of SoSE started about 2008 with a seminal paper by Judith Dahmann et al. on four different forms of SoSs [77].

CONCLUSION

The study of complexity, complex systems, and complex systems engineering is quite fascinating, especially when attempting to push the limits of current understandings in the field. Although multifarious technical aspects abound, this work goes well beyond traditional methods that tend to concentrate on technologies and conventional systems engineering activities. Indeed, when people are intentionally included in systems to be improved or developed, we realize how much further our efforts need to roam and expand toward productive ends that might truly make a positive difference in our lives.

Now, presumably, that you have slogged through this introductory tutorial on the subject, you should be well prepared to embark on the next two chapters of this book. Chapter 2 is about how the *practice* of what we call complex systems engineering leads toward useful *theories*, and Chapter 3 is intended to stimulate organizational *investments* that promise significant benefits to *humanity*.

ACKNOWLEDGMENT

I am grateful to many inspirational and supportive leaders, former co-workers and colleagues, and several current friends for getting me started in the complex field of endeavor represented by this chapter, in particular; for teaching, helping, and working with me to make contributions; and for stimulating me to keep trying to influence our collective way forward toward better understandings. A few names that come to mind are Mike Kuras, Doug Norman, Yaneer Bar-Yam, John Boardman, Al Grasso, Joe DeRosa, George Rebovich, Sarah Sheard, Beverly McCarter, James Martin, and Alex Gorod. Thank you all!

REFERENCES

1. White, B. E. (2007) "Systems Engineering Lexicon." Author's consulting service web site. http://cau-ses.net/.
2. Ashby, W. Ross (1956) "Requisite Variety." Chapter 11 of *An Introduction to Cybernetics*. London: Chapman & Hall. *Introduction to Cybernetics*.
3. Boardman, John, and Sauser, Brian (2008) *Systems Thinking – Coping With 21st Century Problems*. Boca Raton, FL: CRC Press.
4. Checkland, Peter (1999) *Systems Thinking, Systems Practice – Soft Systems Methodology: A 30 Year Perspective*. New York: John Wiley & Sons.
5. Hardin, G. (1968) "The Tragedy of the Commons." *Science*. Vol. 162. pp. 1243–1248. doi:10.1126/science.162.3859.1243. PMID 5699198.
6. Norman, Douglas O., and White, Brian E. (2008) *"So...,"* asks the Chief Engineer *"What do I go do?"* 2nd Annual IEEE Systems Conference. 7–10 April 2008. Montreal, Quebec, Canada. 8 April 2008.
7. Rechtin, E. (1991) *System Architecting: Creating and Building Complex Systems*. Englewood Cliffs, NJ: Prentice Hall. p. 284.
8. Taleb, Nassim Nicholas (2012) *Antifragile – Things that Gain from Disorder*. New York: Random House.
9. de Weck, O., and Eckert, C. (2007) "A Classification of Uncertainty for Early Product and System Design." ESD-WP-2007-10. Working Paper. Engineering Systems Division. Massachusetts Institute of Technology. Cambridge, MA. February 2007.
10. Mikaelian, Tsoline (2009) "An Integrated Real Options Framework for Model-based Identification and Valuation of Options under uncertainty." Ph.D. Dissertation. M.I.T. June 2009. http://dspace.mit.edu/bitstream/handle/1721.1/51676/501814018.pdf.
11. Bartolomei, Jason E. (2007) "Qualitative knowledge construction for engineering systems: extending the design structure matrix methodology in scope

and procedure." Ph.D. Dissertation. M.I.T. http://dspace.mit.edu/handle/1721.1/43855.

12. Ross, Adam Michael (2007) "Managing unarticulated value: changeability in multi-attribute tradespace exploration." M.I.T. Dissertation. http://dspace.mit.edu/handle/1721.1/35089.

13. Maier, Mark W. (1998) "Architecting Principles for Systems-of-Systems." *Systems Engineering.* Vol. 1, Issue 4. pp. 267–284. Article first published online: 9 February 1999. DOI: 10.1002/(SICI)1520-6858(1998)1:4<267::AID-SYS3>3.0.CO;2-D. Copyright © 1998 John Wiley & Sons, Inc. http://onlinelibrary.wiley.com/doi/10.1002/(SICI)1520-6858(1998)1:4%3C267::AID-SYS3%3E3.0.CO;2-D/abstract.

14. Carlock, Paul, and Lane, Jo Ann (2006) "System of Systems Enterprise Systems Engineering, the Enterprise Architecture Management Framework, and System of system Cost Estimation." Center for Software Engineering. University of Southern California. usccse2006-618. November 2006.

15. Helbing, Dirk (2012) "Agent-Based Modeling." Chapter 12. *Social Self-Organization.* New York: Springer. pp. 25–70. http://link.springer.com/chapter/10.1007/978-3-642-24004-1_2.

16. Agent-based model." Wikipedia. The Free Encyclopedia. (Accessed 18 May 2020) http://en.wikipedia.org/wiki/Agent-based_model.

17. Forrester, Jay W. (1989) "The Beginning of System Dynamics." Banquet Talk. International Meeting of the System Dynamics Society. Stuttgart, Germany. 13 July 1989. http://web.mit.edu/sysdyn/sd-intro/D-4165-1.pdf.

18. Churchman, C. W. (1979) *The Systems Approach.* New York: Dell Books.

19. Gorod, A., White, B. E., Ireland, V., Gandhi, S. J., and Sauser, B. J. (2015) *Case Studies in System of Systems, Enterprise Systems, and Complex Systems Engineering.* Boca Raton, FL: CRC Press, Taylor & Francis Group.

20. Rebovich, George, Jr., and White, Brian E. (2011) Eds., *Enterprise Systems Engineering – Advances in the Theory and Practice.* Boca Raton, FL: CRC Press.

21. Various Authors (2000) "Industrial automation systems – Requirements for enterprise-reference architectures and methodologies." Geneva, Switzerland: International Organization for Standardization (ISO). ISO 15704:2000.

22. FEAF (1999) *Federal Enterprise Architecture Framework (FEAF).* Washington, DC: Chief Information Officer (CIO) Council.

23. MODAF (2004) "Ministry of Defence Architecture Framework (MODAF)." Version 2. London, U.K.: Ministry of Defence.

24. Giachetti, R. E. (2010) *Design of Enterprise Systems: Theory, Architecture, and Methods.* Boca Raton, FL: CRC Press: Taylor & Francis Group.

25. Extended Enterprise (2013) http://www.businessdictionary.com/definition/extended-enterprise.html. (Accessed 19 May 2020).

26. Dyer, L. and Ericksen, J. (2009) "Complexity-based agile enterprises: Putting self-organizing emergence to work." Wilkinson, A. et al., Eds. *The Sage Handbook of Human Resource Management.* London, U.K.: Sage. pp. 436–457.

27. Stacey, R. (2006) "The science of complexity: An alternative perspective for strategic change processes." R. MacIntosh, et al., Eds. *Complexity and*

Organization: Readings and Conversations. London, U.K.: Routledge. pp. 74–100.

28. Martin, J. N. (2010) "An Enterprise Systems Engineering Framework." 20th Anniversary International Council on Systems Engineering (INCOSE) International Symposium, 12–15 July 2010. Chicago, IL.

29. Rouse, W. B. (2009) "Engineering the Enterprise as a System." Sage, A. P., and Rouse, W. B., Eds. *Handbook of Systems Engineering and Management.* 2nd Ed. New York: Wiley and Sons, Inc.

30. Rouse, W. B. (2005) "Enterprise as Systems: Essential Challenges and Enterprise Transformation." In *Systems Engineering.* Vol. 8, No. 2. pp. 138–150.

31. Lawson, H. (2010) *A Journey Through the Systems Landscape.* Kings College, UK: College Publications.

32. SEBoK (2014) "Enterprise Systems Engineering Background." Guide to the Systems Engineering Body of Knowledge (SEBoK). 2014. http://www.sebokwiki.org/wiki/Enterprise_Systems_Engineering_Background (Accessed 19 May 2020).

33. Meadows, Donella, Randers, Jorgen, and Meadows, Dennis (2004) *Limits to Growth – The 30 Year Update.* White River Junction, VT: Chelsea Green Publishing Company.

34. White, B. E. (2013) "Applying Complex Systems Engineering in Balancing Our Earth's Population and Natural Resources." The 7th International Conference for Systems Engineering of the Israeli Society for Systems Engineering (INCOSE_IL). Herzlia, Israel. 4–5 March 2013.

35. Stout, Martha (2005) *The Sociopath Next Door*, New York: Broadway Books (Random House).

36. Hawking, Stephen (1996) *A Brief History of Time.* New York: Bantam Books.

37. Wilber, G. F. (2009) "Boeing's SoSE Approach to e-Enabling Commercial Airlines." In M. Jamshidi, Ed. *System of systems engineering – innovations for the 21st century.* New York: J. Wiley & Sons.

38. DoD (2003) "DoDAF V2.0, (2003)." DoD Architectural Framework Version 1.0. The Deskbook and Volumes I & II. Department of Defence Architecture Working Group. Superseded by DoDAF V 1.5.

39. Maier, Mark W., and Rechtin, Eberhardt (2009) *The Art of System Architecting.* Appendix A. Third Edition. Boca Raton, FL: CRC Press. pp. 395–408.

40. Crawley, Edward, de Weck, Olivier, Eppinger, Steven, Magee, Christopher, Moses, Joel, Seering, Warren, Schindall, Joel, Wallace, David, and Whitney, Daniel (2004) *The Influence of Architecture in Engineering Systems.* Engineering Systems Monograph. Engineering Systems Division. (ESD) The ESD Architecture Committee. M.I.T. 29–31 March 2004. http://esd.mit.edu/symposium/pdfs/monograph/architecture-b.pdf.

41. Dahmann, Judith (2009) "Systems engineering for Department of Defence System of Systems." M. Jamshidi, Ed. *System of systems engineering – innovations for the 21st century.* New York: J. Wiley & Sons. pp. 218–231.

42. Gharajedaghi, Jamshid (2006) *Systems Thinking – Managing Chaos and Complexity: a Platform for Designing Business Architecture.* 2nd Ed. New York: Butterworth-Heinemann.

43. Dagli, C. H., and Kilicay-Ergin, N. (2009) "System of Systems Architecting." M. Jamshidi, Ed. *System of systems engineering – innovations for the 21st century*. New York: J. Wiley & Sons. pp. 77–100.

44. Azani, C. H. (2008) "System of Systems Architecting via Natural Development Principles." *International Conference on System of Systems Engineering*. Singapore. 2–4 June 2008.

45. Khoo, T. (2009) "Domain Engineering Methodology." IEEE SysCon 2009. 3rd Annual IEEE International Systems Conference. Vancouver, Canada. 23–26 March 2009.

46. Meilich, A. (2006) "System of Systems (SoS) Engineering & Architecture Challenges in a Net Centric Environment." IEEE/SMC International Conference on System of Systems Engineering. Los Angeles, 24–26 April 2006.

47. Bjelkemyr, M., Semere, D., and Lindberg, B. (2007) "An Engineering Systems Perspective on System of Systems Methodology." Ist Annual IEEE Systems Conference. Honolulu, Hawaii. 9–12 April 2007.

48. DeLaurentis, D., and Crossley, W. (2005) "A Taxonomy-based Perspective for System of Systems Design Methods." IEEE System, Man, & Cybernetics Conference. Waikoloa, Hawaii. 10–12 October 2005. Paper 0-7803-9298-1/05.

49. Sheard, Sarah (2012) "Assessing the Impact of Complexity Attributes on System Development Project Outcomes." Ph.D. Dissertation. Stevens Institute of Technology. Hoboken, NJ.

50. Ramalingam, Ben, Jones, Harry, Reba, Toussaint, and Young, John (2008) "Exploring the science of complexity ideas and implications for development and humanitarian efforts." London: ODI. Working Paper 285.

51. Robert Rosen, Robert (1991) *Life Itself: A Comprehensive Inquiry into the Nature, Origin, and Fabrication of Life*. New York: Columbia University Press.

52. Jervis, R. (1997) *System Effects: Complexity in Political and Social Life*. Princeton, NJ: Princeton University Press. Mason and Mitoff (1981).

53. Mitleton-Kelly, Eve (2003) "Ten Principles of Complexity and Enabling Infrastructures." Eve Mitleton-Kelly, Ed. *Complex systems and evolutionary perspectives on organisations – The Application of Complexity Theory to Organizations*. Bingley, UK: Emerald Group Publishing Limited.

54. Kauffman, Stuart (1993) *Origins of Order: Self-Organization and Selection*. New York: Oxford University Press.

55. Pinker, Steven (2009) *How the Mind Works*. New York: W. W. Norton & Company.

56. Waldrop, M. (1994) *Complexity: The Emerging Science at the Edge of Order and Chaos*. London: Penguin Books.

57. Westley, F., Zimmerman, B., and Patton, M. Quinn (2006) *Getting to Maybe: How the World is Changed*. Toronto: Random House.

58. Marion, Russ, and Uhl-Bien, Mary (2003) "Complexity Theory and Al-Qaeda: Examining Complex Leadership." *Emergence*. Vol. 5, No. 1. pp. 54–76.

59. Capra, F. (1996) *The Web of Life*. London: Flamingo/Harper Collins.

60. Stacey, R. (1995) *Complexity and Creativity in Organisations*. San Francisco: Berret-Koehler Publishers.

61. Plowman, D. A., Solansky, S.T., Beck, T. E., Baker, L. T., Kulkarni, M., and D. V. Travis, D. V. (2007) "The role of leadership in emergent, self-organization." *The Leadership Quarterly*. Vol. 18. pp. 341–356.

62. Plowman, D. A., Baker, L. T., Beck, T. E., Kulkarni, M., Solansky, S. T., and Travis, D. V. (2007) "Radical change accidentally: The emergence and amplification of small change." *Academy of Management Journal.* Vol. 50, No. 3. pp. 513–541.

63. Knowles, Richard N. (2002) *The Leadership Dance – Pathways to Extraordinary Organizational Effectiveness.* 3rd Edition. The Center for Self-Organizing Leadership. Niagara Falls, NY.

64. Uhl-Bien, N., Marion, R., and McKelvey, B. (2007) "Complexity Leadership Theory: Shifting leadership from the industrial age to the knowledge era." *The Leadership Quarterly.* Vol 18, No. 4. pp. 298–318.

65. McCarter, Beverly Gay, and White, Brian E. (2013) *Leadership in Chaordic Organizations.* Boca Raton, FL: CRC Press.

66. Cilliers, P. (1998) *Complexity and postmodernism: Understanding complex systems.* New York: Routledge.

67. Marion, R. (1999) *The Edge of Organization: Chaos and Complexity Theories of Formal Social Systems.* Thousand Oaks, CA: Sage.

68. Kauffman, Stuart (1995) *At Home In The Universe – The Search For Laws Of Self-Organization And Complexity.* New York: Oxford University Press.

69. Dawkins, Richard (2006) *The Selfish Gene.* 30th Anniversary edition. Oxford: Oxford University Press.

70. Haberfellner, R., and de Weck, O. (2005) "Agile Systems-Engineering versus Agile-Systems Engineering." INCOSE Symposium. Rochester, NY. 10–15 July 2005.

71. Baldwin, C., and K. B. Clark, K. B. (2004) "Modularity in the design of complex engineering systems." https://www.mendeley.com/?interaction_required=true.

72. White, B. E. (2001) "Layered Communications Architecture for the Global Grid." Military Communications Conference (MILCOM). McLean, VA. 20 October 2001.

73. White, B. E. (2007) "On Interpreting Scale (or View) and Emergence in Complex Systems Engineering." 1st Annual IEEE Systems Conference. 9–12 April 2007. Honolulu, HI. 11 April 2007.

74. Bar-Yam, Yaneer (2005) *Making Things Work – Solving Complex Problems in a Complex World*, 1st Edition. NECSI Knowledge Press.

75. Norman, D. O., and Kuras, M. L. (2006) "Engineering Complex Systems." *Chapter 10. Complex Engineered Systems – Science Meets Technology.* Braha, D., Minai, A., and Bar-Yam, Y., Eds. New England Complex Systems Institute. Cambridge, MA. Springer.

76. B. E. White, B. E. (2008) "Complex adaptive systems engineering." 8th Understanding Complex Systems Symposium. University of Illinois at Urbana-Champaign, IL. 12–15 May 2008.

77. Dahmann, Judith S., Rebovich, George, Jr., and Lane, Jo Ann (2008) "Systems Engineering for Capabilities." *CrossTalk, The Journal of Defense Software Engineering.* Vol. 21, No. 11. November, 2008. pp. 4–9.

Evolution of Practice — Theory of Complex Adaptive Systems Engineering

2

"We cannot solve our problems with the same thinking that we used when we created them."

> — *Albert Einstein, quoted in CityLab.com [re: complexity]*
> — *(The Week, 20 April 2018, p. 17)*

INTRODUCTION

A generally accepted theory of complex adaptive systems engineering (CASE) still does not exist despite decades of effort by protagonists, e.g., Yaneer Bar-Yam [1] and various systems engineering (SE) practitioners [2–11]. Those of us deeply immersed in advancing CASE have come to realize that its practice must continue to evolve for a while yet. This is evidenced from many case studies [12] that illuminate how we are still learning about complex adaptive systems. This ongoing process is expected to continue for several more years before a generally accepted theory underpinning practical experience is established.

This chapter covers a number of topics, reflecting attempts to advance the variety of stakeholders' understanding in this field of endeavor. These detailed topics include complexity and its characteristics, complex systems (CSs) and their behaviors, complex systems engineering (CSE) and its principles, and a comprehensive CASE methodology [13], all that can be usefully applied to advance the development or creation of a CS. Keep in mind that these topics are highly interrelated and complementary.

COMPLEXITY AND COMPLEX SYSTEMS

This section covers some of the basic ideas of complexity and systems that are considered complex. Generally, the simplest form of complexity is complication; complexity is an unbounded continuum that begins with complication. Considering various complexity characteristics and CS behaviors, discussed below, the more that apply, the more complex the entity. Keep in mind that these characteristics and behaviors apply to any system but with varying degrees of intensity. Perhaps it is fruitless, at least for the time being, to attempt to usefully quantify a particular degree of complexity.

We will also provide several examples of CSs, whether they be "just" systems, one of the four varieties of system of systems (SoS), so-called enterprises, or the most general kind of system, CSs, cf., Figure 1.1b of Chapter 1. Also, keep in mind the nested hierarchy among these system labels as indicated by this figure.

Upcoming examples of real-life CSs operating in today's world may enrich your appreciation of the more theoretical portions of this book. We encourage connecting the ideas expressed here to actions we might collectively make toward progress in solving challenging problems many of us are facing.

In this context, systems satisfy the following rather broad definition. System: An interacting mix of elements forming an intended whole greater than the sum of its parts. *Features*: These elements may include people, cultures, organizations, policies, services, techniques, technologies, information/data, facilities, products, procedures, processes, and other human-made (or natural) entities. The whole is sufficiently cohesive to have an identity distinct from its environment [14].

Complexity Characteristics

Strictly speaking, highly CSs are truly unique in that no exact replicas exist or can be reproduced. CSs are difficult to define. It is better to think of them as having no fixed boundary. Rather, one needs to discuss the possibility of a fuzzy boundary and try to decide where it may lie. These systems are unpredictable and have (unexpected) emergent properties. By definition, deterministic systems are predictable, but usually one cannot easily foresee what happens many iterations in advance without actually experiencing them. That is, even though each successive iterative step is well defined, if there are too many steps, the ultimate result is essentially impossible to know in advance. CSs continually evolve at several different scales that need to be viewed concurrently, to the extent possible, to improve system understanding. Although a CS may reach points of relative stability at times, it will soon move on, fluidly reaching and passing through other states. Such systems are self-organized, collaborative, and adaptive. They are open to exchanging energy and information with their environment and are heavily interdependent on the multifarious interactions of the component portions of the system. They tend to be inefficient in terms of carrying extra baggage comprising diverse capabilities but effective as a whole. "Healthy" CSs are very robust and can become even stronger in the presence of relatively small and random perturbations that induce some stress, so as to better face future threats.

Some characteristics of complex entities, viz., CSs, are listed in Table 2.1. Some effort was made to list the characteristics in order of decreasing importance in terms of characterizing CSs. However, in most cases there is not much difference in impact between characteristics listed adjacently. The more of these characteristics that apply, the more complex the system. These characteristics will be highlighted and briefly expanded upon in the following paragraphs. Please understand and remember that these characteristics are overlapping, complementary, and not independent of each another.

Uniqueness: In a more or less global and abstract sense, one might consider any set of CSs to be essentially the same, e.g., human beings, in that they all seem to have the same essential characteristics. However, when contemplating our particular "view" of a complex entity, viz., its scale, granularity, and timeframe [15,16], for example, along with a more flexible "mindsight," [17] we can better appreciate how different the instance can

TABLE 2.1 Characteristics of Complex Systems

#	Characteristic	Comment by Way of Explanation
1	Unique	Irreproducible and no other exact copies exist
2	Ambiguous	Ill-defined/shifting boundary and content
3	Unpredictable	Cannot foresee or pre-specify outcomes
4	Emergent	Unexpected results; multiple scales involved
5	Evolutionary	Concurrent/continual development/operations
6	Unstable	Transitory, largely nonhierarchical structure
7	Self-organized	Highly interactive and re-integratable
8	Collaborative	Thrives on cooperation/competition
9	Experimental	Explores/tests new possibilities
10	Adaptable	Learns from/responds to current conditions
11	Open	Influenced by and influences environment
12	Inter-relational	Long-range effects but short-ranges dominate
13	Robust/inefficient	Depends on diversity but effective holistically
14	Anti-fragile	Strengthened by small random perturbations

be within its underlying reality. By delving deeper we can understand the uniqueness.

Ambiguity: Try defining a CS precisely and share that definition with a friend or colleague. Isn't it likely that there would be significant disagreement worthy of discussion? This results from the likelihood that everyone has at least a slightly different perception of things and that by sharing ideas, we can collectively achieve a better understanding of the underlying reality that none of us can describe without some inescapable imperfection(s). In particular, the exact content and boundary of the evidently ill-defined CS are often debatable.

Unpredictability: With simpler CSs we can sometimes determine with less uncertainty what may happen because our knowledge of the CS is detailed enough. But the vast majority of CSs are unpredictable because the natures of their inherent makeup, inner workings, and interactions with their environments are largely mysterious. Even an entirely deterministic system, i.e., whose next state is completely determined by its current state and input (s), can be largely unpredictable if one tries to postulate its state and output(s) far enough in the future, e.g., after hundreds of thousands or millions of iterations, admittedly sufficiently beyond current capabilities in computational volumes and speeds.

Emergence: Those that believe in predictable emergence may be employing the wrong meaning of the word emergence; it seems more correct to insist that emergence only applies to the unexpected [15,16]. Indeed, those surprises that cannot be completely explained rationally after the fact are the most intriguing. With CSs it is next to impossible, even employing different scales (or more generally, views), to fully explain what portions of the CS's interactions within itself and/or with its environment is responsible for the observed result(s).

Evolution: A typical CS is ever changing and developing in response to its self-organization and two-way environmental influences. Thereby it continually develops and evolves, sometimes in concurrence with other CSs with which it interacts. Because of changeability, a CS is rarely, if ever, in a stable state. Any semblance of stability is transitory. If for some unfortunate reason or set of conditions, perhaps resulting from a rigid hierarchical structure, for example, stability occurs, the CS basically is ensnared in statis and certainly not operating at the "edge of chaos" where it is most effective, robust, and possibly anti-fragile [18].

Instability: A CS tends to continually evolve based on internal interactions among portions of itself (whose structure is largely nonhierarchical) and influences from (and toward) its external environment. Thus, the so-called state of a CS is transitory and unstable, although a semblance of stability can persist for a time until the CS moves on.

Self-organization: As should become apparent by now, a "healthy" CS is not very dependent on outside influences for its development. A CS can operate pretty much on its own, thank you. Within the realm of human-made CS creation or improvement, the more effective leaders understand and exhibit the need to stimulate self-organization by advocating for and rewarding those that proactively engage in that type of process. Complex difficulties are most often overcome through self-organization and not from hierarchical, top-down "command and control" dictums that rarely succeed in the more complex situations. Pursuits of emerging opportunities with informed risks can lead to more attractive paths to solutions along with benefits that can be added or re-integrated into the CS's development.

Collaboration: By its very nature, a CS involves and typically thrives on both cooperation and competition not only with the outside world but within itself, among its own component subsystems or systemic portions. This is the fundamental nature of self-organization.

Experimentation: This can be a conscious activity in human-made CSs but is also an inescapable fact of how natural CSs operate, as evidenced by several of the above characteristics. The CS is continually testing additional possibilities.

Adaptability: Throughout its operation a CS is learning from what's happening in the sense that its experiences are driving future behavior. Thus, CSs are inherently adaptive, and that's why the term "complex adaptive system" is essentially equivalent to our nomenclature of CS.

Openness: Too many systems engineers create an impervious "closed" boundary around a given system, primarily to make it easier to engineer and especially so they can more successfully employ classical, conventional, or traditional SE techniques that often do not work well with CSs. Then they wonder why their efforts may be inadequate in the more complex situations. On the contrary, it's important to realize that CSs should be treated as completely "open" and that they can be influenced by unknown events or factors. This realization leads to the need for choosing the boundary of the CS, hopefully with the consensus of those involved, with great care to help ensure that the boundary is large enough to permit effective improvements or solutions but not so large that the latter become nearly impossible.

Relationships: Clearly, multifarious interactions are at play in CSs. The internal ones are difficult to pinpoint in terms of their effects on the holistic behavior of the CS. In contrast, external interactions may become relatively clear, at least from an overall perspective, but these cannot/should not be totally prevented, even if so desired, because of the CS's innate characteristic of openness.

Robustness/inefficiency/anti-fragility: A CS's strength is largely due to the diversity and self-organization of its elements, relationships, and interactions. Although this often makes for inefficiency, as measured by traditional SE methods, diversity is critical in creating or improving the CS's effectiveness, i.e., the more desirable outcome capabilities are achievable. Robustness, i.e., the welcome ability to withstand shocks of various sizes and intensities, is largely a byproduct. In addition, if the CS is somehow protected from the largest, potentially negative ("Black Swan") [19] shocks and subjected to lots of relatively small-shock anti-fragile [18] perturbations, it is likely to become even stronger.

Anti-fragility: A "healthy" CS becomes stronger as it evolves by experiencing and reacting to (and usually overcoming) many small, mostly external (but also internal) perturbations. This process of becoming "anti-fragile" makes the CS not only less fragile (or vulnerable to becoming "unhealthy," approaching stasis, or even dying) but also more resistant to future larger perturbations that might threaten its existence.

Complex System Behaviors

Perhaps the most important behavior is the stimulation of different perspectives in observers of the multiple scales of a CS's evolution. When working in a group, it is critical to try to understand what is happening before taking action. A CS thrives on diversity, self-organization, and freewheeling interactions among the component portions of the system. All this helps organize the many factors at play to ensure robust operation that is quite survivable and adaptable. The system is ever changing, evolving on its own as a whole, and exhibiting emergent properties that are largely unexpected and even surprising. A very slight change of initial conditions can apply quite different results the system operates; this phenomenon is often called the "butterfly effect." CSs generally perform openly, and it is challenging to objectively observe what is happening. This is made even more difficult because most observers are inside the system as opposed to viewing it from the outside. In a fashion analogous to anti-fragility discussed briefly just above, a CS likes to operate at the edge of chaos, i.e., between order and chaos; arguably, this is its most productive region of operation.

Several typical behaviors of CSs (shown in Table 2.2) are next discussed in a little more detail. As with CS characteristics, the more of these behaviors that apply, the more complex the system. And again, note that these behaviors are also overlapping, complementary, and not independent of each another. Here, an effort has been made to reorder system behaviors roughly according to decreasing impact of a given behavior on the others. Nonetheless, as with the system characteristics, there is not that much difference in impact between behaviors listed adjacently.

TABLE 2.2 Complex System Behaviors

#	System Behavior	Comment/Guidance
1	Stimulates different perspectives	Seek understanding
2	Thrives on diversity	Leverage inter-relationships
3	Self-organized	Reward collaboration
4	Internal/external relationships are key	Experiment to learn
5	Acts robustly	Be adaptable/survivable
6	Many factors at play	Build common ground
7	Evolves on its own as a whole	Recognize unpredictability
8	Ever changing	Manage uncertainty
9	Surprising emergence	Expect the unexpected
10	Sensitive to small effects	Mind initial conditions
11	Informs the observer	Try to be objective
12	Exhibits tight and loose couplings	Categorize interactions
13	Performs openly	Carefully interpret causes
14	Operates at edge of chaos	Note where best happens

Stimulates different perspectives: We can gain a better understanding of a CS by viewing it from several different angles and sharing our perspectives. The rather mysterious nature of most CSs should not only motivate but also reward that approach.

Thrives on diversity: Increases in a CS's viability and vitality depend on leveraging the interactions of the self-organized elements of diversity. As with natural evolution and the survival of species, a CS is better able to continue evolving if it can draw upon, as needed, the varying abilities of its subsystem components and inputs from its environment.

Self-organized: See previous comments under CS characteristics. Again, here we emphasize the role of a good leader in ensuring conditions for and rewarding this behavior.

Internal/external relationships are key: In CSs it's all about the interactions within the system and with other (external) systems or the CS's non-system environment. These relationships likely present some constraints but also opportunities that can be cautiously pursued. Much can be learned, sometimes through experimentation, from these endeavors.

Acts robustly: See previous remarks under CS characteristics about robust/inefficient/anti-fragile. This goes a long way toward ensuring the CS can adapt and survive.

Many factors at play: Usually, there is a lot going on. With human-made systems, it's especially important to concentrate, at least at first, with goals/objectives/capabilities about which most stakeholders care. Clearly, resources should be mainly devoted to common concerns, not detailed needs of just a few individuals. Once broadly based needs are met, of course, additional remaining resources can be used to address specific unmet desires.

Evolves on its own as a whole: Remember to emphasize a holistic perspective and be sensitive to observing (unexpected) emergent properties. Realize that predicting what a CS will do, especially in the future (à la Yogi Berra), is often the wrong focus. Do not become frustrated with your likely inability to ascertain what portions of the CS or its environment causes these events. Just concentrate on deciding whether the CS is moving in acceptable, and hopefully desired, directions and plan your potential interventions accordingly.

Ever changing: Start to worry if CS activity slows; this could be a sign of deterioration. Be especially concerned if the CS stops changing; this indicates the possible onset of stasis, i.e., the death of the system. Try to manage uncertainties calmly but with mindfulness. Have a well-thought-through process in place to deal with contingencies as they arise.

Surprising emergence: Although the unexpected should be anticipated, decide which of the emergent events or conditions are truly surprising. Emergent properties should not only be noted, they should be documented for sharing with constituents and stakeholders, as appropriate. Within reason, try to determine what causes the emergence, especially the surprises, but recognize the difficulty in isolating cause and effect.

Sensitive to small effects: Small changes of initial conditions can make a vast difference in the eventual behavior of CSs. This is known as the "butterfly effect," e.g., the flapping of a butterfly's wings in Japan can ultimately result in a hurricane in the Atlantic Ocean! Keep this phenomenon in mind. For example, in attempting to simulate a situation using agent-based modeling, be mindful that very small changes in the rules governing agent interactions can generate very different results.

Informs the observer: CSs generally, or at least should, operate openly, although there is a tendency in human-made systems for those who think they are in charge to strive to hide what is happening, often for selfish reasons, but sometimes to protect intellectual property of competitive advantage. This is certainly understandable. However, we should embrace information sharing for mutual benefit as we build trust with one another. The benefits can far outweigh the risks if this is done with care and wisdom. In any case, we must try to be objective in what we observe to better decide what to do next.

Exhibits tight and loose couplings: From a network point of view, some "nodes" in a CS are probably "visited" more often, perhaps with a cluster of several such nodes, formed in part by relatively short interconnecting "links." Other nodes may be more widely scattered with fewer interconnecting links. Depending on the topic of interest, it is useful to determine the subnetwork that matters most in terms of its relationship to the problem or issue at hand and to largely ignore or abstract out the rest of the network. This can simplify the improvement or solution process by homing in on what one might be able to influence and ignoring that which you probably cannot affect or effect. Of course, if the CS is so nebulous that it cannot be treated as a network, some other approaches must be devised in attempting to categorize the interactions.

Performs openly: See the above comments under informs the observer, evolves on its own as a whole, and surprising emergence.

Operates at the edge of chaos: Although this may sound counterintuitive, this is where you want the CS to operate because this is the region where it is the most vital or "healthy." This is where the CS activities are more engaging and able to create alternative states or conditions that may lead to better performance in the sense you desire. Naturally, as you try to influence the CS to perform even better, you want to temper your interventions so as to prevent the system from going into chaos, where its behavior may be so erratic that you cannot begin to ascertain what, if anything, is happening of import. Clearly, this may be easier said than done. In the meantime, enjoy, as best you can, the more effective operations.

Complex System Examples

Table 2.3 lists a very abbreviated collection of CSs along with a rough attempt, depending on the conditions assumed, to classify, categorize, and associate a few attributes with each, considering the various system types we have been describing, again, cf., Figure 1.1b of Chapter 1. At least one system of each type is shown. Space limitations obviate the capability to elaborate here on this list. Interested readers may contact me at bewhite71@gmail.com for additional detail. Air traffic management is used as an illustration in the next (profilers) subsection.

Many other classes for Table 2.3 and their exemplar instances are omitted here, e.g., a country (Ireland, a CS), finance (the stock market, an enterprise), government (US Congress, a CS), holiday (Thanksgiving, an enterprise), leisure (the beach, a CS), military (Future Combat Systems, a directed SoS), mindsight (patriotism, an enterprise), observance (Ramadan, a CS), politics (Democratic and Republican Parties, enterprises), problem (world hunger, a CS), professional society (International Council on Systems Engineering [INCOSE], an enterprise), religion (Christianity, a CS), retail stores (Walmart, an enterprise), sports (New England Patriots, an enterprise), and unions (International Brotherhood of Teamsters, an enterprise).

With some extra time, you might be intrigued enough to flesh out some of the examples listed above and/or conjure up your own to play with. As you are doing so, keep the definitions in mind and carefully consider what you decide is inside, on, or outside the boundary of your chosen system.

Complex System Profilers

An enterprise systems engineering (ESE) profiler that is adept in helping to characterize a complex problem situation is provided in Figure 2.1 [20]. As a follow-up to the ESE profiler, a systems engineering (SE) activities (SEA) profiler that provides a way of describing what one is doing to advance the practice of CASE is provided in Figure 2.2 [21]. Both these figures are explained and justified below.

First, referring to the ESE profiler of Figure 2.1, the middle, inner, and outer rings on the left refer to the traditional program domain, a transitional domain, and what is called the "messy frontier," respectively, which are briefly described on the right.

To employ this profiler in any given situation of choice, you need to carefully consider each of the 24 entries in the eight sectors of the four quadrants. In every sector the idea is to select, with a dot, say, the most appropriate ring that best describes your situation and then to connect the

TABLE 2.3 Categorization of Various Example Systems from the Real World

System Class	System Entity	System Type	System Attributes
Academia	Harvard University	Enterprise	Historic; top of Ivy League; government source
Aerospace	Orion	Directed SoS	NASA* managed; launching humans into space
Aerospace	The Space Shuttle	Directed SoS	NASA* managed; launching humans into orbit
Company	Ford Motor Company	Enterprise	International; One Team, One Plan, One Goal
Commerce	Commercial Supply Chain	Collaborative SoS	Vendors, shippers, transporters, distributors, buyers
Conglomerate	NBC*	Enterprise	RCA* founded; peacock logo; Comcast; MSNBC*
Conveyance	Boeing 747 aircraft	Directed SoS	Innovative; huge; intercontinental; long-lasting
Corporation	The MITRE Corporation	Enterprise	SE* in public interest; manages FFRDCs*; formed: 1958
Discipline	Economics	Complex system	More difficult than sociology; involves world's markets
Entertainment	PBS*	Enterprise	Higher quality/more educational than most public media
Environment	Climate change	Complex system	Global, ocean warming, chaotic storms/ weather, ominous future
Environment	Renewable energy	Collaborative SoS	Fund research and distribution; reduce fossil fuel dependence

(*continued*)

TABLE 2.3   Categorization of Various Example Systems from the Real World (*continued*)

System Class	System Entity	System Type	System Attributes
Environment	The Earth	Complex system	Development/operation is concurrent and continuous
Field	Engineering	Enterprise	Addresses/solves problems by systemic/ systematic means
Industry	Road vehicle industry	Complex system	Manufacturers, dealers, buying public, and rules of the road
Intelligence	National Security Agency	Enterprise	Funded worldwide information gathering; highly secretive
Living	Healthcare	Complex system	Doctors rewarded for tests; lobbyists dominate drug prices
Methodologies	SE, SoSE, ESE, and CSE*	System	Practice/theories currently less mature as one go to the right
Scourge	International terrorism	Virtual SoS	Global, deadly, mindless, ruthless, fearless, and disorganized
Scourge	Rogue state containment	Complex system	Marginalize China, Russia, Iran, Syria, North Korea, et al.
Security	Cyber security protection	Acknowledged SoS	Pervasive problem, largely *ad hoc* network and political focus
Service	Global Positioning System	Acknowledged SoS	US-led communications, sensor, and automated location app
Service	The Internet	Collaborative SoS	Global independent online systems voluntarily networking

(*continued*)

TABLE 2.3 Categorization of Various Example Systems from the Real World (*continued*)

System Class	System Entity	System Type	System Attributes
Service	The World Wide Web	Virtual SoS	Interlinked hypertext documents accessed via web browser
Society	Social networks	Collaborative SoS	Mitigate bogus content; help kids cope with human interactions
Transportation	Air traffic management	Acknowledged SoS	International operations conducted by FAA,* ICAO,* et al.
Transportation	ADS-B*	Directed SoS	Broadcasts aircraft position, velocity, pilot intent; limited use
Transportation	National Infrastructure	Collaborative SoS	Rebuild/repair roads/highways; improve/expand public options

*Acronyms
ADS-B = Automatic Dependent Surveillance – Broadcast
CSE = Complex Systems Engineering
ESE = Enterprise Systems Engineering
FAA = Federal Aviation Administration
FFRDC = Federally Funded Research and Development Center
ICAO = International Civil Aviation Organization
MSNBC = not an acronym (part of NBC)
NASA = National Aeronautics and Space Administration
NBC = National Broadcasting Company
PBS = Public Broadcasting Service
RCA = Radio Corporation of America
SE = Systems Engineering
SoS = System of Systems
SoSE = System of Systems Engineering

dots, as shown, forming what is called a "spider diagram." The more this diagram extends toward the outer edge of the profiler, the more complex your problem.

For instance, in the hypothetical example of Figure 2.1, five of the eight dots are in the messy frontier, three are in the transitional domain, and none are in the traditional domain. This suggests a quite difficult situation being confronted. This configuration might correspond to air traffic management, for example. Within the Strategic Context, the Mission Environment,

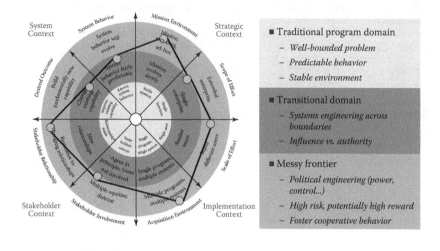

FIGURE 2.1   Enterprise Systems Engineering Profiler.

Typical Systems Engineering Activity	Left End of Slider		Center Intermediate Interval	Right Intermediate Interval	Right End of Slider
Define the System Problem	Establish Requirements	Re-Scope to Changed Requirements	Revise & Restate Objectives	Postulate Future Enterprise Needs	Discover Needed Capabilities
Analyze Alternatives	Do Systems Tradeoffs	Model/Simulate System Functionalities	Perform Systematic Cost-Benefit Analyses	Include Social & Psychological Factors	Emphasize Enterprise Aspect
Utilize a Guiding Architecture	Apply Existing Framework	Develop Architectural Perspectives (Views)	Really Define Architecture	Allow Architecture to Adapt	Use Evolutionary Architecture
Consider Technical Approaches	Employ Known Techniques	Research & Plan for New Technologies	Research & Evaluate New Technical Ideas	Pursue Promising Techniques	Experiment & Innovate
Pursue Solutions	Choose Only One Approach	Consider Alternative Solution Approaches	Investigate Possible Departures from Plan	Iterate & Shape Solution Space	Work to Keep Options Open
Manage Contingencies	Emphasize and Manage Risks	Mitigate Risks & Look for Opportunities	Identify & Manage Uncertainties	Pursue Enterprise Opportunities	Treat Unknown Unknowns
Develop Implementations	Try Ideas Off-Line	Prepare Enhancements for Fielding	Play in Operational Exercises	Develop in Realistic Environments	Innovate With Users Safely
Install Operating Capabilities	Test Needed Functionalities	Work Towards Better Interoperability	Advance Horizontal Integration	Advocate for Needed Policy Changes	Consolidate Mission Successes
Learn from Field Effectiveness	Analyze & Fix Problems	Propose Operational Effectiveness Measures	Collect Value Metrics and Learn Lessons	Adjust Enterprise Approach	Promulgate Learning

Traditional Systems Engineering (TSE)   Aggregate Assessment of Above Slider Positions   Complex Systems Engineering (CSE)

FIGURE 2.2   Systems Engineering Activity Profiler.

containing multifarious flying objects including airliners, general aviation aircraft, drones, birds, etc., is very fluid and *ad hoc*; the Scope of Effort required suggests an extended enterprise that includes among other entities, the flying public. Clearly, the Implementation Context contains a Scale of Effort consisting of many different users, and an Acquisition Environment of multiple programs and systems. The Stakeholder Context includes Stakeholder Involvement of many that at least agree in principle on air safety, for example, although some stakeholders may not be directly involved, and a Stakeholder Relationship characterized by some that may resist changing relationships. Finally, the System Context consists of a Desired Outcome that will essentially change existing capability and a System Behavior that is fairly predictable. All these selections are judgment calls, of course.

Ideally, the instantiation (spider diagram) of your profile is created by consensus through discussions among of your project/program team members, managers, and leaders. If not, further debate about different dot placements might be warranted until consensus is reached. It is important to not abandon this process prematurely, for a thorough understanding of the problem is critical before pursuing potential solutions because sufficient time and effort spent up front will often mitigate future schedule delays and cost overruns.

This profiler can also be used in discussions with other projects/program teams to compare and contrast their perceptions of the problem. This can be helpful to all such groups grappling with similar issues of a given domain.

Second, turning now to the SEA profiler of Figure 2.2, Column 1 contains nominal descriptions of nine typical activities involved in almost any SE project/program, and these are listed in a logical although not necessarily systemic order. You can use the rectangular "sliders" to describe what you're actually doing about the problem characterized by the ESE profiler. Naturally, this requires careful consideration of the individual descriptions within the five columns of the nine rows of the SEA profiler. The idea is to place a given row's slider in one of the seven equally spaced discrete positions between the second and sixth columns of each row. The further to the right, a slider position, the more complex is your action in addressing that particular aspect of the problem. The analogue slider position at the bottom of the profiler is used to reflect the collective or average position of the nine sliders depicted above.

The two sets of slider positions shown in Figure 2.2 are representative of two past attempts to modernize air traffic management communication and surveillance. The left and right sets, respectively, had to do with creating international standards for (1) an integrated digital voice and data communication system between pilots and air traffic controllers and (2) the automatic dependent surveillance broadcast (ADS-B) system where each aircraft would transmit its position, velocity, and "tail number" periodically so that other pilots could "see" them on

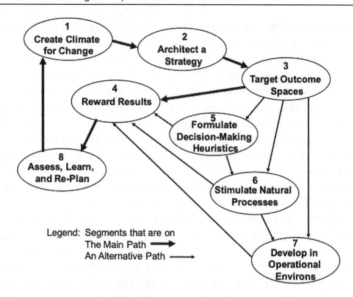

FIGURE 2.3 Early Version of CASE.

their cockpit instrumentation. For more detail see the subsequent instantiation of these two example activities associated with Figure 2.3 and Table 2.4.

Again ideally and to the extent possible, slider positions should reflect consensus of the team. If not, it is quite likely that at least some of the activities currently being pursued may be inadequate toward making sufficient progress to alleviate the problem at hand. In such cases, the team may recognize a need for more productive approaches and the appropriate sliders could be subsequently moved to the right to reflect more vigorous actions. Also, this profile can be shared with other teams for mutual benefit.

Stakeholders

Ways of effectively dealing with CSs have been promoted for several decades. Although significant progress has been made, several important challenges remain. A basic challenge that still needs to be overcome involves identifying key stakeholders struggling with CSs and convincing them to try adopting promising methodologies.

Identifying and dealing with stakeholders is a huge topic in itself, and one can even consider an architecture focused on stewarding stakeholder relationships [22]. Convincing stakeholders of anything is highly dependent on

TABLE 2.4   Complex Adaptive Systems Engineering Activities

#	CASE Activity	Description
1	Create climate for change	Create a climate for engineering the environment of the system. Continually plan for agile, constructive change (accelerating the processes of natural evolution) through proactive dialogue with stakeholders, especially customers.
2	Architect a strategy	For the system, within its various system, system of systems (SoS), enterprise, and/or CS contexts.
3	Target outcome spaces	Describe the customer's mission/vision in terms of one or more desired outcome spaces, *not* solutions.
4	Reward results	Work with the customer and a governing body to create appropriate incentives.
5	Formulate decision-making heuristics	Discover and promulgate management heuristics that will help the customer better know *how* and *when* to make decisions.
6	Stimulate natural processes	Continually "stir the pot" by introducing variation (innovation) and selection (integration) while shaping and enabling future constructive change and trying to avoid chaos and stasis, respectively.
7	Develop in operational environs	Create a bias for developing evolutionary improvements of the system in actual operational environments with real users.
8	Assess, learn, and re-plan	Continually evaluate overall results and trends focusing on the "big picture" and revisit all the above activities in an iterative fashion to improve their application.

your ability to gain their trust and understanding through allowing yourself to be somewhat vulnerable by sharing information, not only of a business nature but also personal stories. This is closely related to the fundamental and highly successful leadership trait of "leading with heart," [23] where you should endeavor to build stronger relationships by becoming personally known to and knowledgeable about your colleagues.

Another fundamental challenge is discovering fertile environments in which to experiment with methods for improvement. An organization's workplace is one place to start. Care should be used in first approaching more receptive individuals in selecting relatively small arenas to try out new or alternative methods. Depending on the degrees of success, these experiments can be expanded upon, particularly if others become aware of resulting benefits. If you are not part of a formal organization, working as an independent consultant, for example, almost any existing or prospective client might present opportunities for progress.

Then there is the challenge of conducting and documenting case studies that help establish what works and what does not seem to help make a difference [12]. One should be on the lookout to stimulate such work in the interest of furthering the worthwhile cause of CSE.

COMPLEX SYSTEMS ENGINEERING

CASE Methodology (Early Version)

An early version of a CASE methodology is depicted in in the flow chart of Figure 2.3; it included activities described more fully in Table 2.4.

This early version of CASE is relatively easy to grasp by contemplating the potential order in applying the "bubbles" of Figure 2.3 and absorbing their respective meanings as described in Table 2.4. Keep this depiction in mind until an updated and more elaborate version of CASE is presented in a later section of this chapter.

Although a step-by-step qualitative process is suggested by CASE, there is very little, if any, quantification offered and much room for interpreting the meaning of each step or stage of the process. To the extent this seems dissatisfying, understand that this largely reflects the strength of the methodology as it can be applied to many situations. Creating examples of its application is the business of case studies that can and should be quite specific and will usually contain a fair amount of quantitative data and information.

Next the *original* version CASE methodology is applied to air traffic management examples [24,25].

Activity 1: Create Climate for Change

In the mid-1990s, The MITRE Corporation, in operating one of its Federally Funded Research and Development Centers (FFRDCs) — the Center for Advanced Aviation Systems Development (CAASD) that supports the Federal Aviation Administration (FAA) — was involved in an approximately four-year effort to modernize air traffic control (ATC) air-ground communications between pilots and controllers.

A healthy climate for change was already established by the even-then recognized need to provide more capacity in the 25 kHz-wide channels allocated to ATC communication.

Air traffic at major airports was expected to increase, and existing communications capacity was predicted to be exhausted within about seven years around several metropolitan areas, especially New York City. Thus, readiness to change was driven by this impending threat.

The ensuing RTCA (formerly known as the Radio Technical Commission for Aeronautics) and International Civil Aviation Authority (ICAO) meetings became self-organizing venues. In quadrupling the communications capacity, we collaborated and shared many experiences and learnings in creating a widely acceptable digital waveform.

Along the way we thoroughly explored innovation and integration options while considering inter-channel, co-channel, and aircraft co-site radio interference tradeoffs, for example.

Activity 2: Architect a Strategy

Consider trying to improve the air transportation system in just one component, say, the communications system between pilots and air traffic controllers. The aforementioned attempt in the 1990s to introduce a fully digital, integrated voice-data radio capability had only limited success because the system boundary was not inclusive enough.

An ICAO waveform standard was achieved [26], but the entire system (VHF Digital Link [VDL] Mode 3) was not implemented because of inadequate support. Air traffic controllers were reluctant to modify existing procedures. The European ATC association (EUROCONTROL) wanted another round of analogue channel splitting. The airlines balked at yet another new radio. The FAA was unable to secure congressional funding for the ground radios, and so on.

Greater success might have been achieved by engaging more closely with all these stakeholders early — treating them as part of the system. In other words, a better strategy should have been architected — in the beginning of the effort.

Activity 3: Target Outcome Spaces

In contrast, technology is *not* the limiting factor in modernizing air transportation in the United States. For instance, the air-ground communications

VDL Mode 3 radios (of the previously mentioned ICAO standard) and in-cockpit situational awareness, ADS-B systems represent mature technologies.

Other problems involving people, processes, and business tradeoffs have thus far prevented the widespread introduction of these subsystems into the air traffic management system. Outcome spaces need to include these entities!

Activity 4: Reward Results

An especially difficult case would be trying to visualize how "reward results" would work for all stakeholders in ATC and air traffic management. Now may be an even better time to experiment in limited ways under the FAA's Next Generation Air Transportation System (NextGen) effort [27].

Activity 5: Formulate Decision-Making Heuristics

Americans used to wonder whether *yesterday's* pervasive airline delays and largely nonexistent airline profits could have been mitigated by taking earlier action on modernizing the ATC system in the United States. It's curious that dire predictions of running out of airport capacity within seven years or so were still being made in 2008 just as emphatically as 10–15 years before that! We wondered whether this was "crying wolf" again, thus resulting in less motivation to continue pushing for modernization.

Happily for the airlines, they seem to have improved their profit situation without our help, at least, by increasing ticket prices; charging for food on board; and imposing heavy baggage, rebooking, and cancellation fees.

Or perhaps it is time to wait no longer and to think about transforming air transportation in the United States safely rather than focusing so much on effectiveness and efficiency.

For example, greater emphasis on sharing military and civilian air traffic management resources (e.g., air traffic controllers and funding) and assets (e.g., air bases, airports, and aircraft) might lead to a larger outcome space of creative solutions benefitting multiple stakeholders.

Some much better "rules-of-thumb" are needed for decision makers in this domain!

Activity 6: Stimulate Natural Processes

An example of Activity 6 is the experimentation with ADS-B using MITRE's Universal Access Transceiver (UAT) in the challenging (because of prevailing bad weather and rugged terrain) air traffic environment of general aviation (GA) users in Alaska [28].

What better environment (where there have been many small aircraft crashes) might be used to demonstrate the value of ADS-B for improving safety? The FAA successfully created worldwide interest through this competing system concept, instigated in part by providing free radio equipment to GA users [28]. Thus, MITRE's compelling experiment really stimulated renewed worldwide attention toward implementing ADS-B.

Activity 7: Develop in Operational Environs

Although the CAASD-invented User Request Evaluation Tool (URET) was conceived in the laboratory, it matured in the field; it was used in the Indianapolis and Memphis Air Route Traffic Control Centers (ARTCCs) from November 1997 through 2008 and has since been installed nationwide.

URET enhances the ability of air traffic controllers to foresee potential aircraft conflicts many minutes in advance. This allows enough time for pilots to take corrective action without significantly disrupting flight times or sacrificing passenger comfort.

Activity 8: Assess, Learn, and Re-Plan

NextGen is an example of learning from past efforts in the air traffic management arena. In a larger context, the FAA joined with several other government agencies under the Joint Planning and Development Office (JPDO) to modernize air transportation in the United States.

Complex Systems Engineering Principles

As in any serious discipline, it is advisable to have a set of principles to guide the effort. Some CSE principles are summarized in Table 2.5. They are elaborated upon as follows [29].

Elaborating somewhat on the above-listed principles and actions:

1. Bring Humility. Attempt to suppress hubris in trying to quickly solve the problem; instead, devote considerable effort to better understand the problem by gathering facts and speaking with experienced practitioners within the domain of interest.

   Human-made CSs should be thought of as including people, intentionally. Doing this, we realize that no one can be in full control of the CS nor be able to accurately predict what will happen as the CS evolves. Therefore, we must bring a healthy dose of

TABLE 2.5   Some Complex Systems Engineering Principles

#	Principle	Action Suggested
1	Bring humility	Acknowledge shortcomings and seek understanding
2	Follow holism	Focus on whole enterprise rather than just pieces
3	Achieve balance	Shun optimality but improve overall capabilities
4	Utilize trans-disciplines	Apply effective techniques of related domains, e.g., see just below
5	Embrace nontraditional aspects	Define enterprise boundary considering political, operational, economic, moral, etc., domains
6	Nurture discussions	Listen to others and reward information sharing
7	Pursue opportunities	Take informed risks in pursuing alternative solutions
8	Formulate heuristics	Devise rules of thumb and improve decision taking
9	Foster trust	Brave personal vulnerability in gaining help from others
10	Create interactive environment	Open and facilitate meaningful interchanges
11	Stimulate self-organization	Nurture, reward, and celebrate collaborations
12	Seek simple elements	Deal with most pervasive common concerns
13	Enforce layered architecture	Establish early powerful guide to progress
14	Elevate future goals	Endeavor with others to help solve world problems

humility in attempting to engineer the CS, e.g., the SoS or enterprise, and its environment. Humility especially helps in understanding each other's terminology, which permits us to accelerate progress or at least move forward, i.e., we don't need to fully agree on definitions or our use of words to usefully get on with the job.

2. Follow Holism. Concentrate on the whole enterprise and the interactions among its components and with the environment. Unless the problem is just complicated (the simplest form of complexity), avoid the usual SE approach of reductionism and constructionism;

these techniques are fine in simpler situations but only when they apply!.

One should not use reductionism (exclusively) to accomplish your goals. By the time one subdivides the problem, works on optimizing each resulting subsystem, and reassembles the parts, the complex system and its environment have moved on, and little will perform as desired. This is a fundamental problem with government system acquisitions that take many years to accomplish. Many times, overly ambitious weapons programs get cancelled but only after billions of dollars have been expended [24]. With complex systems, systemic thinking is more appropriate than systematic thinking [30]. Constructivism is more *a propos* (holistic) in the present systems age than reductionism (a piece-part approach) of the past machine age.

3. Achieve Balance. Rather than trying to optimize the parts or even the whole, instead be mindful of achieving balance among competing enterprise aspects to improve overall capabilities.

Optimization of CSs may be impossible in a mathematical sense. Optimizing subsystems can detract from the potential efficacy of the whole. Rather, try to balance various subsystem thrusts. In an automobile enterprise if manufacturing and sales are each rewarded by the most cars, either more cars will be produced than can be sold, or so many cars will be sold that manufacturing cannot keep up. Reward collaborations that keep manufacturing and sales abreast while increasing both production and sales.

4. Utilize Trans-Disciplines. Learn from other, perhaps widely separated, domains.

Most engineers think of SE as multidisciplinary, with the fields of sensing, information processing and computing, communicating, networking and the hard sciences of physics and mathematics coming together. But in CSE people are considered part of the system. They are difficult, if not impossible, to model or control. Hence, "trans-disciplines," namely, the soft sciences, like philosophy (!) (e.g., [2]), psychology, sociology, organizational change theory, economics, and politics, should be considered. [2] is a great book that well informs CSE!

5. Embrace things like POET (political, operational, economic, as well as technical, domains and aspects) in defining the enterprise's (often "fuzzy") boundary while keeping the big picture and the most important aspects in mind.

Let's face it. In the world's most pressing problems, politics and economics play critical roles, in addition to operational procedures and technical means. CSE must deal with all four aspects or results will be unsatisfactory. One may devise a great technical solution that could improve operations, but this will not go anywhere without (political) acceptance from stakeholders. Understand your stakeholders' values to establish win-win scenarios. Someone also needs to agree to pay (economically) for the improvements.

6. Nurture Discussions. Share relevant information (leaders should reward and not punish this!) to garner different points of view so that, collectively, there is a better understanding of the problem's underlying reality and the enterprise's agreed-to boundary.

   First realize that every person sees things differently [16]. No one has an exclusive grasp of the truth about CS. Better solutions are attained through leveraging a large group's cognitive diversity than by a panel of experts [31]. In SE we spend too much time arguing over definitions instead of seeking to understand how we use words. Only after this mutual understanding is attained can a group make real progress.

7. Pursue Opportunities. Enterprise opportunities often abound, and they should be pursued while staying informed of potential associated risks. If one only identifies and tries to mitigate risks (as is typical in traditional SE), attractive solutions that might be found by exploring alternative paths could be missed.

   It is evident that there has been a great emphasis (e.g., in the US Department of Defense [DoD]) on identifying and mitigating risks — but largely at the expense of largely ignoring opportunities that are at least as important as risks. In a CS (such as a military enterprise) the principal risk is not pursuing opportunities [32]. Yet a balance must be struck. With many opportunities, initial expectations of a profitable business relationship can be too high. When visiting a new company, what if grass is taking over the parking lot? Share impressions of potential prospects in meetings but don't give away all your advice (especially your intellectual property) for nothing. If successful, no task needing attention is too small; it could lead to other opportunities. Do whatever it takes if necessary.

8. Formulate Heuristics. One way of helping decision makers make better decisions is to recall, develop, or propose good heuristics. Sometimes postponing decisions works well because more information is available on what is happening with previous interventions.

   Knowing when to make what decisions is a formidable challenge in managing uncertainty. Those in authority must make important decisions, at least occasionally, because that is part of their job.

Some excellent work has been accomplished in formulating heuristics, i.e., rules of thumb, to help decision makers [9]. Nevertheless, heuristics is still a fertile research area. System dynamics was invented by Jay Forrester of MIT by 1968. [33, p. 208] Here the importance of time delays is tantamount. What initially might apparently be positive effects from your system intervention(s) may ultimately prove to be negative, and vice versa. Insist on believable credentials (a simple heuristic) before engaging. Ask oneself, do they really get it? Even if there is no burning platform, are they in enough pain because their things are not working to be willing to break their mold and try something different? Heed early signs involvements are not gelling. Follow-up to reaffirm first impressions and note whether promises are made good. Although the author uses heuristics in this relatively "narrow sense," broader definitions exist, e.g., "ways of generating solutions to problems" and "techniques and tools for making improvements" (31, pp. 7, 22). This book is also highly recommended.

9. Foster Trust. One engenders trust by increasingly sharing information that is reliable and safe in both directions. It takes courage to show personal vulnerability in sharing, but the prospect of gaining greater understanding from others' knowledge should be worth it.

How can one expect to interact with stakeholders productively without mutual trust? Establishing trust is difficult, takes a lot of time, and can be lost immediately if a precipitous event is handled badly. It is imperative to share information or progress will suffer. Do not adopt the usual mantra that information is power nor follow most organizational cultures of protecting information or get punished. Instead, try sharing business information, albeit to a limited extent at first. If this is echoed so you learn more, great! Then share more and more.

10. Create Interactive Environment. An interactive environment is critical in facilitating meaningful interchanges.

Leaders should not try to drive solutions from the top, for they cannot know just what to do. Instead, continually strive to establish and maintain conditions (e.g., a vision of cooperative interactions and suitable reward structures for doing so) to ensure informed, vigorous, and sustained engagements among the troops. If people play nicely, remarkable improvements are more likely than under autocratic rule. If there is more conflict than competition and collaboration, then either the leader has failed to convey the vision or the incentives are inappropriate and need to be modified.

Responsibilities to act and be responsive are important to embrace. Don't follow rules slavishly but don't fight the system, especially about what you cannot even influence. It may be worthwhile to solicit the inputs of external observers as a check on the organization's direction and/or degree of success.

11. Stimulate Self-Organization. Those leaders and managers in charge should stimulate self-organization by creating attractive conditions for collaboration, competition, and cooperation.

A hallmark of CS is self-organization among its living elements. This is particularly true in natural complex systems such as beehives, anthills, bird flocks, fish schools, etc. Human languages also strongly self-organize based on how people talk. The powerful human rights demonstrations in the Middle East of early 2011 were self-organized (using social networking).

12. Seek Simple Elements. Concentrate on those things that everyone cares about rather than relatively minor "stovepipe" concerns. This can create compelling simplicity within complexity that can achieve results that have widespread benefits such as horizontal interoperability.

Another property of many CSs in nature is the simplicity of the participating elements. Speaking of beehives and anthills, for example, one can be amazed at what they accomplish within their very robust societies when each worker bee or ant seems so limited in capabilities. Imagine what humans might do when they interact in self-organizing ways! One difficulty with our intended SE solutions to complex problems is the size and complexity (or maybe just complication) of the individual pieces. We might better design down-scale and assemble arrangements of smaller identical units that are good at adapting.

13. Enforce Layered Architecture. The early building of a guiding architecture that does not change much compared to the system being developed is recommended. To the extent possible, the architecture should be layered to be more assured of simple and stable interfaces between layers.

Layering is applied to increase flexibility or introduce system improvements following changes in environment or implementation technology, for example. What might be better realized in software in one era is better done in hardware in the next, and vice versa. Each layer is confined to a set of closely knit basic functions, grouped in categories of applications, networking, communication links, or physical implementations. The interfaces between layers are kept simple and stable.

However, the realization within a given layer can be (more often) adapted to different conditions. As long as the interface(s) to that layer remain unchanged, the system still operates effectively.

14. Elevate Future Goals. Look to the future, hopefully with appropriate incentives, so as to reach for more ambitious achievements and even greater success in solving world problems that could benefit all humankind.

What higher goals might one's organization aspire to? Sell the benefits (internally and externally) of devoting a larger share of existing (or even additional) resources toward these moral imperatives.

All the foregoing in this chapter, the complexity characteristics and behaviors, the CS profilers and CSE principles, etc., are next integrated to form the latest version of the CASE methodology.

CASE Methodology (Latest Version)

What follows is a detailed elaboration of an updated version of the CASE methodology [13], which contains the following activities [25].

1a – Changing Mindsights

A principal concern associated with the practice of SoS engineering (SoSE) is having a proper mindsight conducive to significant progress in complex domains. Traditional SE mindsets focused on requirements, reductionism, optimization, etc., will not work well in the more difficult situations usually associated with CSs. Mindsight is used to convey a more flexible attitude that is established and modified by embracing multiple perspectives of the underlying truth on which CSE is based. Through self-organized collaborations, including exchanges of individual views, a much better understanding of the problem and what to do about it is likely.

1b – Understanding Persistent Problem

As emphasized in the Soft Systems Methodology (SSM) [4], better understanding the (presumably persistent) problem can be viewed as the primary goal. However, each level of understanding can and should trigger intervening action in an attempt to improve the situation. But problem understanding is a continual process that gets re-exercised after (eventually) observing the result of each intervention. Again, in SoSs, reaching mutual understanding across the SoS, especially among component system organizations, is not easy. Thus, this form of collaboration also warrants extra effort in establishing sustainable SoS mechanisms and pathways for this purpose.

2a - Balancing Opportunities and Risks

Traditional SE is focused too much on risk mitigation. With CSs it is all about opportunities because the system is continuously evolving whether one intervenes or not. Of course, when pursuing opportunities in hope of more productive pathways to good solutions, it is advisable to do this only with an informed risk plan. Leaders should reward those that seek improvements in this way, even if they are unsuccessful at first. One needs to protect against Black Swans [19] but also stimulate anti-fragile development [18]. Clearly, some risk mitigation efforts concerned with avoiding bad things can lead to opportunities that promise good things, and vice versa. The most important principle to observe is balancing opportunities and risks. Maintaining reasonable balances among various competing factors, instead of separate sub-optimizations, is fundamental in SoSE. One way of ensuring SoS adaptability is to put into place, in advance, a shared management process that can be exercised when unexpected events occur.

2b - Mounting Organizational Efforts

Simple problems can often be addressed by individual efforts on a more or less *ad hoc* basis. More often than not, complex problems require additional effort, usually of an organizational variety, typically involving multiple organizations. Good leaders, faced with serious problems, are able to envision, formulate, negotiate, and eventually obtain buy-in participation from relevant organizations, including their own, that can potentially contribute to problems' solutions. Initial goals include creation of an interorganizational structure that is flexible and resilient enough to assure, to the extent possible, continual effort from each organization involved.

2c - Evaluating Stakeholders

There are certainly many stakeholders in a typical SoS, not only because of the SoS level and environment participants but also due to those involved with the component systems. As with simpler systems, it is advisable to identify, assess, and evaluate all the key stakeholders to determine who will assist, resist, and oppose or just need to be informed of the effort and progress. Those stakeholders that are supportive must be continually nurtured, and those against the effort must be neutralized or at least marginalized. Clearly psychology, sociology, organizational change management, politics, economics, ethics, and morality are relevant trans-disciplines that need to be applied.

2d – Postulating Desirable Outcome Space

One of the initial tasks of the SoS leadership is to establish an overall vision or mission for the SoSE team. This should be something that is compelling and internalized to motivate and enable daily personal assessments to the extent common cause contributions have been made. Early on the team must establish desirable outcome spaces and measures so that it will be clear whether postulated solutions developed later fit into at least one of these spaces. At this stage it is premature to focus on specific solutions and their possible outcomes. As the SoSE effort proceeds, these outcome spaces need to be continually adjusted in a fashion analogous to a vehicle's headlights in moving down a road; one does *not* want the scope to be so narrow as to miss opportunities for good solutions, nor so wide that the solution challenge is far too great.

3a – Building Team and Resources

The inter-organizational structure is leveraged initially to locate, consider, select, and assemble talented and/or qualified individuals that will compose the team. Identify, qualify, and obtain other material and financial resources to support the effort. Important processes are planned and emplaced to assure a methodology for dealing with unanticipated events. The smooth and inevitable transition of alternative staff members into/out of the program for various good reasons must be recognized. Sensitivity to external developments and outreach to others that may usefully become involved is also important.

3b – Deciding System Boundary

Contrary to most traditional SE approaches, and perhaps many of those of SoSs, the boundary of a CS is usually very fuzzy. Boundaries must be decided thorough discussions while trying to understand the problem and exercising other CASE activities already discussed. Rationale: If the boundary is too restricted, then it is unlikely that the real problem will be solved; if too ambitious, then the difficulties in achieving improvement escalate exponentially. One fruitful technique for establishing a working SoS boundary by consensus would be to assemble and conduct discussions among a relatively small number of representatives from the SoS level of each system component, hopefully a subset of key stakeholders each of whom have authority to commit to actions on behalf of their organizations. Once an appropriate boundary is decided, it should be made known to the rest of the SoSE team and their affiliates to help guide their collaborative work. Further, it should be agreed that the boundary might be adjusted from time to time based on future events.

3c – Creating Anti-Fragility [18]

First the SoSE team should endeavor to protect the SoS from catastrophic events that may occur, albeit rarely [19]. Suppose, for example, the primary approach is no longer viable because of unforeseen events. Then one of the backup approaches that the team has carried along may become primary. Also, on a smaller scale, it is good engineering practice to focus on what might not work, or what might go wrong, and have a fallback position involving subsystem redundancy, or whatever. Traditionally, SE generally assumes everything will work as intended, but this is a flawed assumption with CSs [34]. Once such protections are in place, the SoSE team should subject the SoS to small random perturbations that can increase its resilience, robustness, and strength. An example: ensure that acquisition contracts are broad enough to admit a wider selection of vendors, increase competition, and offer opportunities to pay for results instead of perceived promises. This is another way of "stirring the pot" to help ensure the best results.

3d – Adjusting Incentive Structures

People tend to behave in ways that are strongly correlated with how they are measured and rewarded. In some SoS environments, particularly those involving military system acquisition, many stakeholders in charge of SoS programs are short-term oriented because they change jobs every two to three years in pursuing career promotions and are not accountable, after being reassigned, for what happened on their previous assignments. This CASE activity is to advocate for, and hopefully help achieve, positive changes in incentive structures to better facilitate leadership styles that create (1) conditions for self-organization, bottom-up efforts, and discourage autocratic, hierarchical, top-down approaches; (2) informed risk taking in pursuing promising opportunities; and (3) more integrated career accountability.

4a – Stimulating Self-Organized Collaborations

Early in any process for confronting a problem and seeking improvement, self-organizational efforts are appropriate. Someone, a leader and/or a manager, is put in charge. An initial action team is assembled. Resources are provided or requisitioned. An overall vision/goal for problem resolution is established. During this time, it is important to establish a healthy spirit of collaboration among the participants to help facilitate (1) information sharing; (2) building trust; (3) developing individual perceptions, viewpoints, and opinions; (4) cooperation; and (5) competition. Collaboration is the heart of what enables the self-organization progress critical to deal effectively with the situation, i.e., achieving a solution. This is especially difficult in SoSs, for the component systems have their own organizations, each of which naturally resists routine collaboration with other organizations because self-interest naturally dominates the affinities with SoS objectives.

4b – Establishing Architecture

The most critical guide to SoSE is a good architecture. The architecture should be established early in the program as a result of significant effort that essentially guarantees a reasonably stable architecture that does not change much compared to the SoS being engineered. Of course, the architecture should be modified, as appropriate, in response to emergent properties or other unexpected events that may indicate the need to change direction. In some architectural frameworks, there is a great temptation to create architectural "views" describing certain perspectives to "check a box" required by management. This is fraught with danger if the views are promulgated before the underlying architecture has been fully developed.

5a – Proposing Specific Interventions

There are many occasions when the SoSE team is almost ready to try something else to help the SoS advance in the desired direction. These actions should be viewed as interventions that have uncertain outcomes because one cannot pre-specify or predict exactly what will happen in a true CS. Prior to implementation the team should propose each intervention to key stake-holders to obtain their reactions, which may lead to some alteration in the plans. Some additional modeling and simulation (M&S) may also be indicated. Finally, before fully committing to a path, some experimentation would also be advisable.

5b – Brainstorming Potential Approaches

Brainstorming is a too casual term for this important activity, but it conveys proper meanings. Here the SoSE team, hopefully in a high-performing, collaborative state, shares ideas about how the problem might be solved, mostly from a technical point of view. However, they must still be mindful of the non-technical aspects, considering all the trans-disciplinary areas that apply. As in normal brainstorming, the free flow of ideas should run its course before anyone on the team attacks any particular idea. Then the more evaluative phase begins, where the offered ideas are criticized, rejected, retained, or refined. The remaining potential approaches should all fit within the agreed vision/mission, desired outcome space, and system boundary. Finally, there should be decisions on which approaches to pursue most vigorously or bring along with lesser degrees as backup options.

5c – Helping Decision Takers

"Takers" is better word than "makers" because taker indicates a more proactive attitude in making difficult decisions. In an SoS, decision taking is more complex because of the larger number of stakeholders involved, across the SoS level and its environment, and among the subsystems. Typically, in CSs, decision makers take decisions too early rather than waiting longer to better evaluate the situation. Quite often there are significant time delays, due to multiple interactions within the CS and with its environment, before the result of the last intervention becomes apparent. Thus, part of the help is to better advise decision takers to wait until a decision time is more evident. More generally, advisors need to provide decision takers with good heuristics (practical rules of thumb) to improve decision taking. An example heuristic indicating the need for some sort of decision, for any key decision taker within the SoS, would be when any component system or subsystem seems to be deemphasizing the SoS in favor of its own system more than might normally be expected.

6a – Modeling and Simulating Behaviors

After the SoSE team has selected a few viable approaches, an analysis of primary alternatives phase begins. M&S includes standard ways of augmenting theoretical analytical capabilities. However, in the case of CSs where people are considered part of the system, intentionally, one can benefit from a complementary form called agent-based modeling. In essence, this involves postulating a small set of rules that autonomous, independent agents follow while interacting with other agents within their hypothetical system environment. An SoS provides a particularly rich opportunity for this, considering the large number and various types of stakeholders at play. Thousands of iterations including tens or hundreds of agents can be run with only modest memories and computational power. Chances are that much can be learned from the behavioral results that emerge from these exercises. The agent rules can be modified to add or subtract rules while seeing which rule sets seem most effective in illuminating what happens. As in more traditional M&S activities, the outcomes inform the SoS development or improvement.

6b – Experimenting with Users

Again, because of uncertainties associated with most SoSs, the SoSE team should experiment with promising ideas in multiple venues. Rather than confining these experiments to laboratory environments typical of traditional SE efforts, one should embrace practitioners and experiment with users in the field, as it were, to the extent possible. Users know better what is needed operationally, and much progress can be made by leveraging their expertise and experience. This is much better than developing something in a "vacuum" or "throwing it over the wall" and having users reject or misuse the supposedly additional capability. However, these operational type experiments must be done safely, so that no one is put in jeopardy.

6c – Taking Appropriate Actions

CSs operating where they should, at the edge of chaos, continue to evolve whether one intervenes or not. That is why, before taking further action, decision takers should objectively observe what is happening over some period of time, as previously mentioned. Interventions are necessary; after all, that is what decision takers are expected to do. These actions should be taken in the spirit of pursuing an opportunity while being informed of potential risks, again, as already discussed. Whatever actions are taken within an SoS, it is quite appropriate to tell other key stakeholders at the SoS level, within the SoS environment, and across all the component systems or subsystems. Then they have increased abilities to consider their own actions to hopefully improve the SoS situation. This sharing of information is *not* so typical in traditional SE environments, where it seems that most are punished, rather than rewarded, for sharing information across organizations.

7 – Measuring What Happens

Fundamentally, the SoSE team must be interested in results that fit into the desired SoS outcome space. There should already be measures in place to better determine whether outcomes fall within that desired space. Better yet, each measure should include metrics that are easily available for gathering relevant data. For example, component system or subsystem managers might report their contributions to the SoS level along with why they think each contribution will fit into the SoS's outcome space, and those instances would be recorded and shared. Some care should be expended to be assured that whatever data gathered are actually used to help avoid wasting resources.

8 – Assessing Results

Here the main challenge may be in reaching consensus across the SoS as to whether improvements have indeed been made. The key stakeholders within any component system or subsystem may not agree on the relative tradeoffs between their local objectives and those of the SoS level stakeholders. Stakeholders within the environment of the SoS but not directly engaged in the SoS should also be consulted to see whether they have noticed improvements. If the SoS is to provide a public service, progress might also be assessed by (1) conducting limited polls or surveys and (2) contacting selected government officials and lawmakers. A sense of accomplishment would do well toward continuing the improvement efforts.

9a – Adding Incremental Capabilities

Traditional SE focuses on requirements near the beginning of nearly every program or project and continually thereafter. Unfortunately, this focus often must continue because in CSs requirements are incomplete, unclear, unstable, and/or even unknown. In SoSs, it is more realistic to rely on the (presumably already) established vision/mission and desired outcome space in lieu of firm requirements. With each intervention and its aftermath, decision takers assess the extent to which the SoS enjoys additional capabilities — or *not*. If the SoS is moving in the positive direction, the next intervention will target an additional capability. If *not*, action should be taken try something else, perhaps in conjunction with undoing the previous intervention. This process is best viewed as incremental, where one builds a little, tests a little, and fields a little. Gradually, with any luck, the SoS situation improves.

9b – Instituting Lessons Learned

Everyone agrees that learning lessons is a good thing. Sometimes, with pressing needs to get on with other work, lessons learned are given short shrift or even omitted. Be wary of only a modicum of lessons-learned effort at the end of a program or project, e.g., by giving them "lip service" without calling attention to them verbally and/or with documentation; it is not that often lessons are really learned! The essential trick is to retain and, hopefully, institute these lessons not only on follow-on programs but also for new projects where those lessons might apply. Instilling the importance of this activity throughout the SoS is highly advisable. More to the point, a systemic process for collecting SoS-related lessons from all component systems would be a good idea. These could be shared with other SoSs, as well, for the benefit of all.

10a – Rewarding Contributors for Useful Results

This is the most important CASE activity, at least in terms of changing acquisition processes for the better. Too often, programs or projects fail when rewards are given up front or via award fees when very little has been accomplished. There need to be much stronger incentives to ensure desired outcomes are ultimately achieved without having to restart or terminate programs. Reserving rewards for achievement is especially challenging in SoSs where most component system stakeholders would refuse to join the SoS effort without reaping immediate tangible benefits. Clearly, existing incentive structures and reward systems cannot be changed significantly "overnight." However, with enough resolve, governing bodies could improve the system gradually, perhaps over decades, by making sure more funding and other compensations are moved later in the programs to help ensure desired results are achieved. As already mentioned, innovative contracts can be prepared to help accommodate this systemic change of rewarding for results.

10b – Publicizing Progress

Coincident with rewarding for results is the publication of not only the recipients but also the results themselves. These publications need *not* be detailed; they could be like stock market quotes, crude oil and gas prices, or public media reports. This serves another purpose — increasing the motivation of others to invest in accomplishing similar outcomes. Investments by component system or subsystem stakeholders in an SoS are necessary in a systemic process that only rewards results because (1) contractors would not receive up-front funding with contract awards, (2) contractor promises to deliver the "goods" would be recorded and held in abeyance until actual delivery to the field, and (3) only successful contractors would be reimbursed and given bonuses. Those contractors that are successful in this would develop "deep pockets" and be able to continue investing in new projects. The contractors that cannot deliver would "dry up and go away." Individual contributors within organizations tend to be rewarded with raises, bonuses, and promotions only after the fact, so in a sense this natural philosophy is merely being extended upwards.

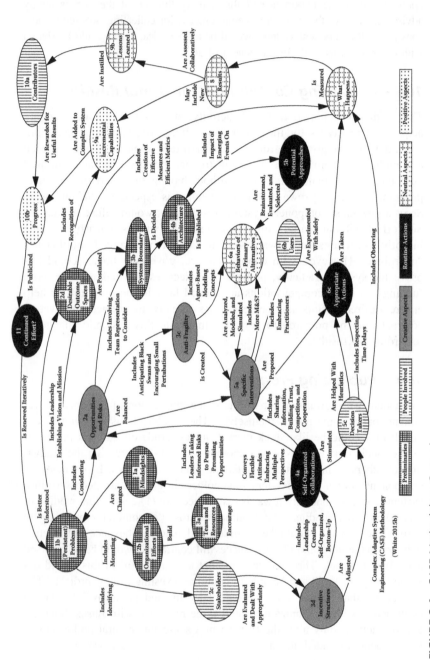

FIGURE 2.4   CASE Methodology Systemigram.

11 – Renewing Continued Effort?

In a "healthy" CS, the work is never done because the system continues to evolve on its own, if nothing else. This has been already well established in Checkland's SSM [4]. One should view CASE as an iterative process that revisits several or all its activities at various times, e.g., during each cycle of activities or after cycling through all activities. The stakeholders of the SoS level should consider renewing the overall SoS at appropriate milestones. It may be necessary to apply renewed effort on some portion of the SoS involving one or more component systems or subsystems. In this case, CASE can be applied again but on a smaller scale.

A systemigram [2] depicting some of the many possible interactions among the above elements is depicted in Figure 2.4.

Here the bubbles are presented in different patterns of black and white to indicate functions of a similar category. Checked black and white stripes are associated with preliminaries, vertical stipes refer to people involved, solid gray to creative aspects, solid black to routine actions, gray and white boxed bubbles to neutral aspects, and dotted bubbles to positive aspects.

We next provide an example of how one might apply the CASE methodology to true CSs. Consider the relatively pervasive problem of the current assault on truth, particularly in the United States.

Example Application of CASE Methodology (Assault on Truth)

In this example, the problem (1b) appears to be one that can be viewed as an increasing assault on the truth where too many people are intent on bolstering their own prejudices and beliefs while ignoring the facts. We choose to take the ideal mindsight (1a) that truth is what should matter most in influencing the human race toward achieving better lives. The truth is at stake in several outcome spaces (2d) where a more desirable acceptance of established facts is clearly needed. For the sake of this argument, we propose the system boundary (3b) to include the domains of climate change, fossil fuel dependence, income inequalities, immigration, misguided spending, national debt, irresponsible politics, lobbying, lust for power, and sexual abuse.

Each of these domains can be viewed as overwhelming, so how can we possibly organize (2b) meaningful efforts to usefully address and hopefully improve the existing situations? One must realize that a guiding architecture (4b) and potential approaches (5b) are required before we attempt to form a motivated team of protagonists and marshal necessary resources (3a) to make meaningful headways.

First, let us assume that we have a few individuals highly motivated to address and understand the problem. A critical early task is to identify and analyze key stakeholders (2c) that have significant actual or potential abilities to influence outcomes. This includes the discovery and awareness of individual incentives (3d) that primarily influence stakeholder behavior. Leadership actions in building support should positively stimulate self-organized collaborations (4a) that will eventually suggest interventions (5a) and ensuing actions (6c) that may result in significant gains in respect for the truth — or not. One needs to observe what happens (7) before deciding (5c) whether the results (8) are acceptable and what lessons might be learned and applied (9b) while instituting whatever incremental capabilities (9a) have been achieved. Contributors (10b) toward any benefits marking true progress (10a) should be publicized and rewarded, but quite likely additional efforts must be mounted to continue the effort (11).

Throughout this endeavor one must be alert for CS opportunities that might be usefully pursued while recognizing associated risks (2a). Various alternatives (6a) should be explored, and the system should be nurtured in ways that might make it stronger to withstand future setbacks (3c).

This discussion reflects just one way the CASE methodology can be traversed and is lacking in content that would undoubtedly arise from an in-depth case study into the assault on truth. However, in attempting to stimulate further treatment of this subject, the author ventures the following opinions.

Scientific evidence and explanations of climate change must be taken more seriously — and soon — to at least mitigate the disastrous effects that are already occurring that threaten large populations [35]. We need to overcome the general resistance to emphasizing renewable energy sources and weaning ourselves away from the eventual unsustainable reliance on oil and coal. Despite what most people of normal and subnormal means believe, the rich — and therefore powerful — tiny minority continues to exacerbate income inequalities. Even with the so-called booming economy, do those in the vast majority really believe they're better off? Immigration has become strictly a racial issue instead of an earlier recognition of gaining strength through diversity. The United States and other rich nations must increase efforts to address root causes of poverty and criminality in countries exhibiting such compelling and overburdening emigrations.

Accelerating national debt exacerbates the depletion of our resource reserves in the form of interest payments. Responsible spending to alleviate social inequities must be accompanied by means to pay for these remedies of injustice. Just when will conservative and liberal politicians come together for the benefit of the public on such issues? It seems that those in power only care about maintaining or increasing such status and thereby cater to lobbyists who live by a profit motive. Then there's the whole category of gay rights, sexual abuse of children, and the denigration of women who somehow — in addition — are not entitled to equal pay for equal work.

When, if ever, will the United States return to its former position of being a model for and the envy of the rest of the world?

CONCLUSION

This chapter is an attempt to convince readers of a more fruitful approach to understanding complex systems, dealing with their consequences, and proactively intervening to try to achieve better outcomes in whatever solution spaces are envisioned. Practice drives theory is the principal thesis. We call for more case studies to help determine what actions seem to work fairly well, consistently, and what activities appear to have little or no beneficial effect.

Rather than continually relying upon or reverting to established systems engineering techniques meant more for less-complex environments, we suggest having the courage to attack difficult problems with greater humility, exploring newer and innovative techniques. The fundamental concept of intentionally including all the key stakeholders in the system to be developed or improved is critical. Otherwise, we may fall into the trap of focusing too much on technology that, although necessary for success, is not sufficient because of the complexity associated with the behavior of people.

Additional efforts that embrace these ideas and expand upon and/or deepen these concepts are encouraged. This author would love to know more about such endeavors.

ACKNOWLEDGMENT

The original version of this chapter was drafted at the invitation of Siddharth Agarwal, lately of Asurion LLC (Nashville, TN) as Senior Manager Product Risk Management & Cybersecurity, who received his 2015 PhD in Engineering Management and Systems under Dr. Cihan H. Dagli at the Missouri University of Science and Technology. The chapter was to be part of a book to be produced by Nova Science Publishers, Inc. Stella Rosa, Administrative Assistant to Nadya S. Columbus at Nova, had suggested that Dr. Agarwal contact me. Unfortunately, an insufficient number of chapters were acquired for that book, so Dr. Agawal suggested I withdraw my chapter, which I did since that gave me an opportunity to publish a slightly revised version here.

REFERENCES

1. Bar-Yam, Y. (2005) *Making Things Work – Solving Complex Problems in a Complex World*. 1st Edition. New England Complex Systems Institute. NECSI Knowledge Press. ISBN 0-9656328-2-2.
2. Boardman, J., and Sauser, B. J. (2008) *Systems Thinking – Coping With 21st Century Problems*. Boca Raton, FL: CRC Press.
3. Carlock, P. and Lane, J. A. (2006) "System of Systems Enterprise Systems Engineering, the Enterprise Architecture Management Framework, and System of system Cost Estimation." Center for Software Engineering. University of Southern California, usccse2006-618, November 2006.
4. Checkland, P. (1999) *Systems Thinking, Systems Practice – Soft Systems Methodology: A 30 Year Perspective*, New York: John Wiley & Sons.
5. Primer (2015) "A Complexity Primer for Systems Engineers." White Paper, International Council On Systems Engineering (INCOSE). https://www.incose.org/docs/default-source/ProductsPublications/a-complexity-primer-for-systems-engineers.pdf?sfvrsn=0&sfvrsn=0. July 2015. Accessed 12 July 2019.
6. Jamshidi, M., Ed. (2009) *System of Systems Engineering – Innovations for the 21st Century*. New York: J. Wiley & Sons.
7. Gharajedaghi, J. (2006) *Systems Thinking – Managing Chaos and Complexity: a Platform for Designing Business Architecture*. 2nd Ed. New York: Butterworth-Heinemann.
8. Hybertson, D. W. (2009) *Model-Oriented Systems Engineering Science – A Unifying Framework for Traditional and Complex Systems*. Boca Raton, FL: CRC Press.
9. Maier, M. W., and Rechtin, E. (2009) *The Art of System Architecting*. Appendix A. Third Edition. Boca Raton, FL: CRC Press. pp, 395–408.
10. Rebovich, G. Jr., and White, B. E., Eds. (2011) *Enterprise Systems Engineering – Advances in the Theory and Practice*. Boca Raton, FL: CRC Press.
11. Rouse, W. B. (2009) "Engineering the Enterprise as a System." Sage, A. P., and Rouse, W. B., Eds. *Handbook of Systems Engineering and Management*. 2nd Ed. New York: Wiley and Sons, Inc.
12. Gorod, A., White, B. E., Ireland, V., Gandhi, S. J., and Sauser, B. J. (2015) *Case Studies in System of Systems, Enterprise Systems, and Complex Systems Engineering*. Boca Raton, FL: CRC Press. Taylor & Francis Group.
13. White, B. E. (2016) "A Complex Adaptive Systems Engineering (CASE) Methodology – The Ten-Year Update." IEEE Systems Conference. Orlando, FL. 18–21 April 2016.

14. White, B. E. (2006) "Fostering Intra-Organizational Communication of Enterprise Systems Engineering Practices." National Defense Industrial Association. 9th Annual Systems Engineering Conference. 23–26 October 2006. San Diego, CA. 26 October 2006.

15. White, B. E. (2007) "On Interpreting Scale (or View) and Emergence in Complex Systems Engineering." 1st Annual IEEE Systems Conference. 9–12 April 2007. Honolulu, HI. 11 April 2007.

16. McCarter, B. G., and White, B. E. (2009) "Emergence of SoS, Sociocognitive Aspects." Chapter Three in *Systems of Systems Engineering – Principles and Applications*, Mo Jamshidi, Ed., Boca Raton, FL: CRC Press.

17. Hawn, G. with Holden, W. (2011) *10 Mindful Minutes*. New York: Penguin Books.

18. Taleb, N. N. (2012) *Antifragile – Things that Gain from Disorder*. New York: Random House.

19. Taleb, N. N., (2007) *The Black Swan – Impact of the HIGHLY IMPROBABLE*. New York: Random House. http://www.amazon.com/Black-Swan-Impact-HighlyImprobable/dp/1400063515/ref=pd_bbs_sr_1/102-6890811-9526543?ie=UTF8&s=books&qid=1192905688&sr=8-1. Accessed 12 July 2019.

20. Stevens, Renée (2008) "Profiling Complex Systems." IEEE Systems Conference. Montreal, Quebec, Canada. 7–10 April 2008.

21. White, B. E. (2010) "Systems Engineering Activity (SEA) Profiler." 8th Conference on Systems Engineering Research (CSER). 17–19 March 2010. Hoboken, NJ. 18 March 2010.

22. McCaughin, L. Keith, and White, Brian E. (2016) "An Architecture for Stewarding Enterprises." IEEE SoSE Conference. Kongsberg, Norway. 12–16 June 2016.

23. Gartland, Tom, with Sweeney, Patrick (2018) *Lead With Heart*. Dallas, TX: BenBella Books, Inc.

24. White, B. E. (2008) "Complex adaptive systems engineering." 8th Understanding Complex Systems Symposium. University of Illinois at Urbana-Champaign, IL. 12-15 May 2008.

25. White, B. E. (2019) "System of Systems (SoS) Engineering." Session 8. "Complex Adaptive Systems Engineering (CASE)." 30 May 2019. Course SYS579. Developed for and provided to Worcester Polytechnic Institute (WPI) for WPI's graduate program in Systems Engineering, Spring, 2019.

26. ICAO (1996) "VHF Digital Link (VDL) TDMA (Mode 3) – Standards and Recommended Practices – Draft," Appendix D to the Report on Agenda Item 4. AMCP/4-WP/70. International Civil Aviation Organization, 4 April 1996.

27. Nextgen (2019) Next Generation Air Traffic Control System (NextGen). Current website: https://www.faa.gov/nextgen/. Accessed: 12 July 2019.

28. Peed, Doyle T. (2009) "Civil Air Traffic Management Surveillance with the Addition of ADS-B and Multilateration Systems – Excerpts from the CNS/ATM Course." The MITRE Corporation. 12 November 2009.

29. White, B. E. (2021) "Enterprise Systems Engineering." *Handbook of Systems Sciences*. 1st Edition. Metcalf, Deguchi and Kijima, https:// www.amazon.com/Handbook-Systems-Sciences-Gary-Metcalf/dp/981150721X.

30. Hester, Patrick T., and Adams, Kevin MacG. (2013) "Thinking Systemically About Complex Systems." Complex Adaptive Systems. Baltimore, MD. 13–15 November 2013.

31. Page, Scott E. (2007) *The Difference – How the Power of Diversity Creates Better Groups, Firms, Schools, and Societies*. Princeton and Oxford: Princeton University Press.
32. White, B. E. (2011) "Enterprise Opportunity and Risk." Chapter 5 in Rebovich, George Jr., and White, Brian E., Eds. *Enterprise Systems Engineering – Advances in the Theory and Practice*. Boca Raton, FL: CRC Press. pp. 161–180.
33. Meadows, Donella H. (2008) *Thinking in Systems – A Primer*. Edited by Diana Wright. Sustainability Institute. White River Junction, VT: Chelsea Green Publishing.
34. Perrow, Charles (1999) *Normal Accidents – Living with High-Risk Technologies*. Princeton, NJ: Princeton University Press.
35. Meadows, Donella, Randers, Jorgen, and Meadows, Dennis (2004) *Limits to Growth – The 30 Year Update*. White River Junction, VT: Chelsea Green Publishing Company.

Leading Change Management to Address Complex World Issues

3

"Whatever we believe about how we got to be the extraordinary creatures we are today is far less important than bringing our intellect to bear on how we get together now around the world and get out of this mess we've made. That's the key thing now. [Never mind] how we got to be who we are."

— Jane Goodall — (Bill Schutt and J.R. Finch, The Himalayan Codex, Bakk Bone, LLC. New York: Harper Collins Publishers, 2017, p. 117)

"There are risks and costs to a program of action, but they are far less than the long-range risks and costs of comfortable inaction."

— John F. Kennedy — (Virginia A. Greiman, Megaproject Management–Lessons on Risk and Project Management from the Big Dig. Project Management Institute. Hoboken, NJ: John Wiley & Sons, Inc., 2013, p. 264)

"Not everything that is faced can be changed. But nothing can be changed until it is faced." — Writer James Baldwin, quoted in Forbes.com —

(The Week, 15 Mar 2019, p. 17)

"In a world as wrong as this one, all we can do is make things as right as we can."

— Novelist Barbara Kingsolver, quoted in The New York Times — (The Week, 28 February 2020, p. 17)

INTRODUCTION

In essence, this chapter is about urging individuals within organizations, e.g., companies, societies, enterprises, etc., to work with their leaders to ensure that each organization meets its *social responsibilities* (italics will be used throughout this chapter for the purpose of emphasis) in helping to make the world a better place in terms of an overarching goal of improving everyone's quality of life. This can only be done if we somehow marshal more available corporate and other private or public resources to address critical humanitarian problems. An excellent definition appears in Wikipedia [1] (see just below) along with several citations and/or references. (In this chapter quotations are usually indicated by uniform indentations as shown here, with any remarks inserted by me shown in brackets [...]; ellipses ... indicate something not shown.)

> Social responsibility is an ethical framework [that] suggests that an entity, be it an organization or individual, has an obligation to act for the benefit of society at large. Social responsibility is a duty every individual has to perform so as to maintain a balance between the economy and the ecosystems. ... [and] sustaining the equilibrium between the two. [This] pertains not only to business organizations but also to everyone whose [actions impact] the environment. This responsibility can be passive, by avoiding engaging in socially harmful acts, or active, by performing activities that directly advance social goals. Social responsibility must be intergenerational since the actions of one generation have consequences on those following.
>
> Businesses can use ethical decision making to secure their businesses by making decisions that allow for government agencies to minimize their involvement with the corporation. ... "self-regulation" rather than market or government mechanisms ... According to some experts, most rules and regulations are formed due to public outcry, which threatens profit maximization [In this book, underlining usually indicates a "click-on" opportunity that can lead to additional information or action, and again, brackets are used within quotes to set off editorial comments (see above)] and therefore the well-being of the shareholder, and that if there is not an outcry there often will be limited regulation.
>
> Some critics argue that corporate social responsibility (CSR) distracts from the fundamental economic role of businesses; others argue that it is nothing more than superficial window-dressing, or "greenwashing"; others argue that it is an attempt to pre-empt the role of governments as a watchdog over powerful corporations though there is no systematic evidence to support these criticisms. A significant number of studies have shown no

negative influence on shareholder results from CSR but rather a slightly negative correlation with improved shareholder returns.

Taking this as a fundamental truth, we will attempt to help determine the extent to which exercising one's social responsibility is beneficial or harmful to business. A number of example instances, mini case studies, if you like, will be discussed that test the premise. The principal question to be answered is this: What responses to social responsibility efforts have been forthcoming that have enhanced organizational objectives, the volume or amount of business, and the associated bottom-line profits? Admittedly, it may well be that despite the considerable effort expended, as detailed below, some readers may decide that insufficient persuasive examples and evidence has been gathered to validate the main premise of this chapter. In these cases we ask for suggestions on what might have been more productive; please take the opportunity to help by contacting me at http://bewhite71@gmail.com. Thank you.

In order to elicit relevant responses from organizations pursuing some aspects of social responsibility, a simple survey was proffered (see the appendix). Each organization's responses, no matter where they resided on a meager to prolific scale, were analyzed, evaluated, and at least summarized in the case studies section. In anticipating the possibility of relatively few in-depth case studies, we also included some laudable role-model examples of humanitarian efforts in the public domain. Later sections of this chapter concern what else might be done to further the social responsibility premise. In the remainder of this introduction, we cite and elaborate upon a few example problem domains particularly identified by public outcry. We then touch on an ecosystem approach, which leads into the next section covering some of the fundamentals of complex systems (such as were explained in Chapter 2) that are essential in providing possibilities for systemic solutions.

Example Problem Domains

Clearly there are some overarching and pervasive world problems such as hunger, homelessness, financial greed, unlimited material growth, lust for power, religious intolerance, terrorism, etc., that must eventually be addressed more effectively or humanity will continue to suffer. However, perhaps it's better to focus on some problem areas that are somewhat less daunting though still considerably challenging from a social responsibility perspective. To name a few, gun violence, social media excesses, the trend toward the erosion of world democracies, and overpopulation and healthcare (which are treated together, with some mention of the COVID-19 pandemic). None of these bodes well for improving our future quality of life.

Gun Violence

Consider the exorbitant pervasiveness of gun violence in the US that is largely nonexistent in other civilized countries. The National Rifle Association (NRA) has been unbelievably successful in preventing common-sense interpretations of the US Constitution's Second Amendment that would reduce profits for gun manufacturers; prohibit gun sales outside legitimate gun stores; outlaw weapons of war for civilian use; improve gun-law enforcement, reporting of suspicious behaviors, and meaningful action in response to tips; expand background checks; raise age limits for buying guns; and provide more funding for mental health screening and treatment. (A logical person might think that guns might be treated similarly by appropriate laws as with motor vehicles, which can also be viewed as potential deadly weapons.) Notably, for example, in response to the public outrage of the 14 February 2018 Parkland, Florida, school massacre, many organizations (as of 20 February 2018 at least, reportedly, about two dozen companies: https://en.wikipedia.org/wiki/2018_NRA_boycott) have terminated their NRA involvements, a very promising development.

In just two weeks after the mass shooting in Nova Scotia, Prime Minister Justin Trudeau banned assault weapons in Canada (see [2] for a short but balanced discussion of this issue), and Australia took similar steps (https://www.opednews.com/articles/Canada-Took-Two-Weeks-to-B-by-Ted-Millar-Assault-Rifle_Assault-Weapon_Assault-Weapons-Ban_Canada-200506-569.html).

> These weapons were designed for one purpose and one purpose only: to kill the largest number of people in the shortest amount of time. There is no use and no place for such weapons in Canada. Effective immediately, it is no longer permitted to buy, sell, transport, import or use military-grade assault weapons in this country.
>
> After the Port Arthur massacre, Australia passed legislation to require licenses to own virtually any type of gun and regulate semiautomatic pistols and rifles as automatic ones.

What more might be done? We suggest that companies and enterprises consider breaking the NRA lobbying stranglehold of Congress by offering Senators and Representative campaign contributions toward enacting remedial gun laws. Alternatively, we can [3] fund "attack ads suggesting pro-gun US politicians support child murder." As stated in a March 2018 op-ed piece, for example, business leaders could make a significant difference in taking meaningful action, as opposed to Congress, public figures, and the media merely sending "thoughts and prayers" to victims and their families and friends [4].

Excesses of Social Media

The detrimental effects of social networks are worth exploring in the context of this chapter. This is very tricky and subtle topic because "absolute" values are difficult (or maybe even impossible) to apply, but as a worthwhile endeavor can we at least continue delving into some of the excesses to expand our awareness? Much can be said about the benefits of social media, which have been significantly enabled by fundamental technological advances, particularly in the 21st century. Billions of people have an amazing array of mechanisms for interacting, communicating, and influencing one another, as well as getting quick access to all kinds of information, just out there but essentially at our fingertips. The speed and spread of data and information by these means are truly remarkable. But what about the largely untapped potential for facilitating among us a better understanding of and wisdom about social issues and what is happening in the world? Many children are addicted to their social media devices to the extent that they minimize personal face-to-face contact not only with parents and other adults but also with their peers. A significant fraction of these children develop psychological problems stemming from lacking more personal social interactions; some have become so disturbed by social media bullying that they have committed suicide [5, 6].

Hordes of people have unconsciously volunteered untold amounts of what should be considered their preferences and private data about themselves via various Internet phenomena, through online shopping with eBay, Amazon, et al.; posting personal information via Facebook, for example; and utilizing Twitter, Google, YouTube, Equifax, etc. It's well within the realm of possibility some day for powerful autocrats to create a 1984-like environment of psychological control [7]. This is already happening in China where the population is subjected to a government-controlled system of scoring one's social acceptability.

Then there is a continual erosion of truth (see previous discussion near the end of Chapter 2, as well as further remarks on getting to the truth near the end of this chapter) exacerbated by those that abuse social media by doctoring content and inserting fraudulent information, as was promulgated by Russian operatives during the 2016 US election process (according to US intelligence agencies) and likely continues. Too many people take such inputs at face value and do not subscribe to a variety of sources as a way of helping to assess the veracity of questionable claims, to say nothing of recognizing pervasive lies. In conjunction with some thoughts about how humans conceive of death, there is this quote (https://www.opednews.com/articles/Death-A-Simple-Idea-with-by-Edward-Curtin-Belief_Coronavirus_Death_Fear-200507-391.html):

In today's electronic mass media world, those who control the mass media that control the narrative flow and the storytelling, control the majority's beliefs and actions.

Also, Voltaire said [8]:

Those who can make you believe absurdities can make you commit atrocities.

Apparently, this non-thinking trend is also continuing based in part on some public polls that rate President Trump and his administration. Some of all this, and more, is aptly summarized in several places, e.g., [9].

Autocratic Regimes, Populism, and Preservation of Democracy

Several Western countries, including France, Germany, the UK, the US, and even Norway, have been plagued by immigration problems in recent decades. The social and economic pressures of millions of refugees trying to escape from intolerable conditions in other countries are intractable, to say the least. For example, the US has millions of undocumented residents whose future is quite uncertain because Congress has failed to enact any new legislation that would lead to citizenship or protect the so-called "dreamers," innocent children who were brought into the country by their parents. Historically, immigration has strengthened the US through the diversity and talents of people seeking better lives and contributing to the workforce and society as a whole. Unfortunately, the politics of these situations are being exploited by populist movements and elected officials who are moving in autocratic directions. This trend is gravely threatening Western democracy. Much needs to be done to accommodate needy immigrants and to help rectify the conditions in their native countries to mitigate their need for emigration.

Overpopulation and Healthcare

Clearly, the continuing expansion of human population, at least in certain areas of the world, is a huge public health (and unlimited material growth [10]) issue. Fundamentally, healthcare service providers and their related agents need to be concerned with not only (1) how best to treat the sick efficiently but also, better yet, (2) our overarching higher moral responsibility in attempting to more effectively *make and keep* people healthy. Preventative healthcare measures are not only moral in themselves but actually save money for the public or private agencies footing some of the bills for healthcare. Rarely, if ever, in public at least, do we concern ourselves with the inconvenient fact of having far too many people to allow either of these outcomes to become completely viable options. Rather, the crucial question is, just how do we balance our responsibilities in providing proper healthcare with creating incentives for limiting population growth that otherwise greatly exacerbates the problem? [11]

The practical challenge of developing healthcare service quality at a global level is immense. Overpopulation is a serious problem generally, and this can severely limit our quality of life [12]; consider ecosystems, for instance [our italics follow]: "... attributes the human-induced loss of biodiversity to three macro phenomena: *increasing human population*, technological change ... and social organization .... Over and above direct exploitation of resources, the primary cause of biodiversity loss ... is habitat destruction as a result of *population growth* and technological change ..." [13, p. 89].

Again, though undoubtedly a controversial and even daring topic, one must sometimes wonder if saving millions of lives is really in the best long-term interest of humankind. Consider how overpopulation and the ecological effects of climate change threaten to drastically decrease our quality of life over many generations. The more cynical view might be to simply acquiesce to the current deplorable situation where too many seem to get sick and die needlessly. This is an especially timely thought in connection with the COVID-19 pandemic. Perhaps President Trump's notorious lack of caring about leading the fight against the virus in favor of ineptly trying to protect his reelection prospects might be viewed rather charitably in that respect. This is in contrast to the Prime Minister of New Zealand, Jacinda Ardern, for instance, who has acted promptly and with insight and compassion in fighting the virus in her country [14] (https://www.theatlantic.com/politics/archive/2020/04/jacinda-ardern-new-zealand-leadership-coronavirus/610237/).

Further, more and more people may lead to greater difficulties in funding proper education to help embolden future generations to counterbalance the current trend toward "Trumpism" in the US and reactionary nationalism in several other countries, as already mentioned above. If the lower and middle classes, as well as women in general, continue to earn relatively less on almost any comparison scale, as robots take over more and more jobs, putting people out of work and making normal jobs and reeducation more difficult to attain [15, 16], the have-nots will be even more unable to afford sending their children to college and may become still angrier at the establishment that they believe is ignoring them [14]. The increased efforts and viability of online learning may help considerably [17].

Ecosystem Approach

The wisdom of taking a broader perspective in complex problems [18] like healthcare, for example, is also emphasized (repeatedly) in [19] again concerning ecosystems, for example:

> Several authors in this book argue for the necessity of multiple perspectives in managing for sustainability. What is implicit in many discussions about incorporation of such perspectives and their translation into governance, however, is that a common worldview (usually some version of scientific positivism) is assumed among participants, even those from different disciplinary or social positions (social activists, natural scientists, [and] economists[, for example]). But what if the collaborators see not only different things in the world, but see different worlds? We wish to extend this discussion further and examine more closely the topic of systems of environmental knowledge and its implications for ecosystem-based management [20, p. 109].
>
> ... [W]hether there are systems of knowledge other than Western science that provide models worth examining [20, p. 111].
>
> ... [I]t would be a mistake to think that only traditional societies can provide information and insights for the ecosystem approach. Any group of people who dwell in an ecosystem have potential contributions to make [20, p. 121].

This is an ethically sound approach when used to improve healthcare services because the complex system inherently functions as an *ecosystem*, which should be thought of as explicitly including people, not just other types of organisms, in the environment. It seems to be commonly believed, in democratic societies, at least, that humans have an innate right to good health. We recognize that health, as a feature of human well-being, is actually an expression of people embodied in the context of "nature," although nature itself certainly does not automatically bestow good health necessarily.

Another manifestation of a worthwhile ecosystem approach is climate change, an additional area presenting an opportunity for moral leadership [4]. What could be more complex than pushing for remedial action against the long-term effects of global warming, particularly in the face of so much political opposition [21], before it's too late? Later we will mention examples of several organizations subjected to our survey that are trying to make a difference in this area, and a few are succeeding.

COMPLEX SYSTEMS

This is a huge topic [21], as it applies to almost everything of human importance that could benefit from a better understanding of complex system (CS) characteristics and behaviors and a more disciplined application of complex systems engineering (CSE) principles that have been developed into a methodology [22]. We briefly summarize some of these precepts (see Chapter 2 for more) here and call for intensified leadership efforts that could stimulate improved management of many of our difficult world problems within the context of our social responsibility mantra.

One would hope that this is what a US President, other heads of state, and their administrations around the world, at least, would possess. Perhaps, then, most of the rest of us would be better able to understand and deal with "unintended consequences" as they undoubtedly arise.

Recognizing CSs Characteristics and Behaviors

No one can be in complete control of a CS, especially those that involve people. The system continually evolves and often exhibits unexpected, emergent properties that cannot be explained solely by understanding the system components. The behavior is holistic and cannot be analyzed, understood, or treated by reductionist (or constructionist) techniques. (Much of this has already been explained in Chapter 2, with the definitions of Chapter 1 as background.) We feel that more of us should believe in and embrace these characteristics as they relate to humans, our environment, and the systems in which we live and that we help create.

Even deterministic CSs can defy prediction in terms of their long-term behavior. Yet CSs behave openly, fostering continual or almost continuous interactions among their components or sub-systems and with their environment. The precise boundary of the system is usually quite fuzzy and can be difficult to define. If the system appears to have stable or semi-stable states, they tend to be quite transitory.

It could be that many of us believe that people often find it psychologically difficult to accept the constantly transitory nature of what they think of as "reality" or "truth." It does take some *humility* (see next section), and a sort of optimism, or at least bravery, in the face of the unknown, to be prepared for the potential realization that in seeking an answer to a question about a complex system, as Gertrude Stein said so well in our opinion (https://www.brainyquote.com/quotes/gertrude_stein_100016):

There ain't no answer. There ain't gonna be any answer. There never has been an answer. That's the answer.

Here are a couple more *a propos* quotes attributed to Voltaire.

> Cherish those who seek the truth but beware of those who find it. https://www.goodreads.com/quotes/76035-cherish-those-who-seek-the-truth-but-beware-of-those
> Doubt is an uncomfortable position, but certainty is a ridiculous one. https://www.saltydoginvestor.com/blog/index.php/doubt-is-an-uncomfortable-position-but-certainty-is-a-ridiculous-one-voltaire/

Instead, one might say, "We don't really know what the hell is going on, but we must keep trying to understand, though we never truly will, and our understanding will keep changing. We must keep trying to do the best we can as we see things at any given time. Nothing will ever be written in stone." Or as Voltaire stated, (https://www.goodreads.com/quotes/580983-life-is-a-shipwreck-but-we-must-not-forget-to)

> Life is a shipwreck, but we must not forget to sing in the lifeboats.

Within the context of this chapter (and book), the best example of a CS is an organization composed of many interacting elements, especially humans, with an open and extensible boundary, e.g., a company, society, or enterprise, etc. The fundamental question here is how can we hope to harness such an organization to increase its effectiveness toward achieving desirable general outcomes and specific objectives in the public (or humanity's) interest?

Applying CSE Principles

Here the reader might review Chapter 2's much more complete list and explanation of such principles.

The first principle is bringing a healthy dose of *humility* to the problem. Everyone must learn to accept the fact that they do not know the entire answer (see previous section) to what makes the CS perform well. People must share their thoughts and ideas, gradually building trust with one another through many iterations, so that collectively a better understanding of the problem and potential solutions are achieved. Even then interventions may not work as expected or hoped, and alternative perturbations may need to be applied. Sufficient time for objective observation is necessary in ascertaining what works and what does not work. Rules of thumb should be posited or developed to help guide the effort that is ultimately and inevitably governed by a few decision takers.

Leadership and Management Roles

We submit that brave leaders are more important than astute managers in CSE. And anyone, exercising their special talents or expertise, for some indeterminate time, at least, can be an effective leader during some aspect of the problem recognition or development of a possible solution. The main tasks of acknowledged leaders (*who have followers*) is to (1) help create a vision that can be internalized by all and (2) stimulate and reward everyone to work together in a self-organized fashion [23] (The reader is encouraged to peruse this rather extensive reference; it is touted as quite readable), along with their managers, to explore *opportunities with informed risk* and hopefully generate a way forward that succeeds in increasing system capabilities; [24] is another fairly complete reference that might be worthwhile to consult.

EXISTING MINI CASE STUDIES

In many domains involving people, there often is an absence of a cogent, well-established, and accepted theory that adequately describes the relevant and important complexities. In such situations, case studies of specific situations can be quite illuminating. Accordingly, we selected a variety of *approximately 140* organizations to query about their humanitarian efforts in an attempt to determine the extent to which we can discover information they are willing to share. Of these, we attempted and were able to contact one way or another (via website, e-mail, or telephone) about 65. The relatively few of these that responded are listed alphabetically in Table 3.1. Some that did not respond are also listed. These shortcomings from our initial anticipated vision in themselves reflect the need for more social responsibility! In most cases we made a website query or e-mail request whose contents are abbreviated in the appendix. In a few cases, via telephone calls, we were able obtain an e-mail address or advice regarding the organization's website. However, we were stymied in a significant number of instances and failed to obtain contact data despite persistent Internet efforts. What may be the final status of our query/request and response activity is also shown in Table 3.1.

Considering the right-most column of this table and unresponsive or tabled entries, we received the following suggestion to consider using in

TABLE 3.1   Organizations Contacted via Website Query or E-Mail Request and Their Responses

Organization	Website	E-mail	Status/Response/Action
Ably Apparel		X	Considered request and Googled information
Advanced Micro Devices, Inc. (AMD)		X	Responded referring to their websites
Apple	X		(https://www.apple.com/ environment/pdf/Apple_ Environmental_Responsibility_ Report_2019.pdf).
Aqua-Aston Hospitality	X	X	Responded quickly with a long list of relevant data, plus three attachments
BAE		X	No response; tabled
Bill & Melinda Gates Foundation	X		Unlikely response because of high volume of requests
Dell			Two chat room sessions were unsuccessful
Equifax		X	"Pleased" to close case without responding
Facebook			Stymied and gave up
Fresenius Medical Care North America			Need to telephone, evidently; tabled
Glenkinchie Distillery		TBD	https://www.tripadvisor.co.uk/ Attraction_Review-g2054927- d558802-Reviews-Glenkinchie_ Distillery-Pencaitland_East_ Lothian_Scotland.html
Green Upward		X	Very new operation so no data; after querying again, the principal provided some very useful thoughts about organizational sustainment.
Houghton Mifflin Harcourt (HMH)		X	myhmhco@hmhco.com; no response; tabled
Hurtigruten Foundation		X	Acknowledged receipt and said they'd respond in due course because of high volume of requests but did not
Illahe Vineyards		X	No response; tabled

(*continued*)

TABLE 3.1 Organizations Contacted via Website Query or E-Mail Request and Their Responses (*continued*)

Organization	Website	E-mail	Status/Response/Action
Kentucky Fried Chicken (KFC)		X	Responded with their website; tabled
The MITRE Corporation		X	No response; omitted firsthand experience
Nike		X	Responded with their website; tabled
PepsiCo			Requested via snail mail but no response; tabled
Raytheon			Requested via LinkedIn but no response; tabled
The Prairie River Network		X	Respondent had no time currently; encouraged for later but did not materialize; tabled

the future under similar circumstances: To grab immediate attention and not just be relegated to the "later" pile, you need to able to "lead" (or begin) your request with a more compelling "elevator pitch," i.e., a good way of grabbing a stranger's attention within the time it takes to ride with them in an elevator. Instead or in addition, lead with the name and maybe a quote or endorsement of a prestigious supporter or organization regarding the value of this study and of the wisdom of expanding it, along with a listing of some of your credentials.

Positive Examples

We start with a few organizations that reflect positive postures and accomplishments.

Ably Apparel

This outfit produces an eco-friendly technology called Filium "that makes any natural fabric repel liquid and resist odor without sacrificing softness or breathability" [25]. Here is what they claim in "Our Story" and "Technology:"

> Along with food and shelter, clothing is one of our basic human needs. And while we might think about how much things cost at the store or complain

about doing laundry or [our] dry cleaning bills, we don't see the hidden costs, like the heavy environmental footprint of clothing production. It's a pretty big deal.

Filium's about more than water resistant clothes. It's a breakthrough that could make a huge impact on the world, in the form of drastically reduced carbon emissions and pollution. It feels good to put on a shirt (or coat or whatever) that not only makes you feel more comfortable, better protected, and ready for anything but also represents a choice that can actually make a difference in the world.

Filium makes ordinary fabrics extraordinary. Imagine a life where your favorite cotton, wool, silk, or linen clothes shrug off water, resist stains, and refuse to smell anything but fresh after weeks of wear.

If you do not already see the indirect benefit of this product from the description above, know that the implication is a greatly reduced need to expend certain resources associated with the usual cleaning of clothes and therefore help protect our environment. This follows an important principle of CSE (see Chapter 2), viz., *utilize POET (politics operations, economics, and technology), define the CS boundary and keep the big picture in mind* [26], to carefully consider the appropriate boundary of your system; sometimes by enlarging the boundary somewhat beyond the immediate obviousness, an attractive possibility presents itself.

Advanced Micro Devices (AMD)

Here are some quotes from AMD's website, https://www.amd.com/en/corporate-responsibility.

> Volunteerism & Philanthropy: For more than 35 years, AMD has invested money, time, and technology in organizations that help strengthen communities worldwide. Additionally, our workforce continues to make their communities a better place by donating their time, talent, and money to charitable causes. Since 1995, AMD's workforce has performed more than 196,000 hours of volunteer service and contributed $16.4M. AMD has a long history of environmental responsibility and transparency. We set ambitions, science-based environmental goals and publicly report our progress. Our goals and programs are designed to minimize environmental impacts in [the] supply chain, across our global building operations, and even to our employees' actions. We have a robust system to manage risks to the environment, and we engage suppliers, customers, investors, and employees worldwide to participate in our sustainability efforts.
>
> Ethics and Compliance: We implement processes to ensure that our practices are consistent with our policies. We believe the integrity of an organization begins with every employee's commitment to our core values and their responsibility to act in concert with those values.

> Product Stewardship: We design innovative technologies that power millions of intelligent devices, from personal computer to cloud servers and more. We strive to create products that improve people's lives while minimizing environmental impacts and energy use.

As we can see AMD is quite a conscientious company. However, it sure would help readers grasp the AMD's impact better, if some more specific examples of what they have done were provided.

AMD appears to exhibit CS behaviors (again, from Chapter 2, highlighted in italics just below) such as *self-organized, thrives on diversity (study inter- and external relationships)*, and *internal* and *external relationships are key (learn from experiments)* with ideas outside their own world.

Apple

In addition to being one of the world's most innovative companies, Apple purports to be environmentally sound, as well (https://www.apple.com/environment/pdf/Apple_Environmental_Responsibility_Report_2019.pdf).

> Creating powerful solutions to push humanity forward takes relentless innovation. Resolving to do this without taking precious resources from the planet means holding ourselves and our suppliers to ever higher standards. We know that accomplishing this work will require all of our best efforts. At Apple, we are committed to building groundbreaking products and services with the mission to leave our world better than we found it.
>
> We strive to create products that are the best in the world and the best for the world. And we continue to make progress toward our environmental priorities. Like powering all Apple facilities worldwide with 100% renewable energy. Creating the next innovation in recycling with Daisy, our newest [still?] disassembly robot. And leading the industry in making our materials safer for people and for the earth. In every product we make, in every innovation we create, our goal is to leave the planet better than we found it. [We obtained this quote from an Apple website earlier but do not recall the URL.]

Apple is widely known for its technological innovation, of course. Most remarkable, perhaps is the almost innate ability, as exemplified by Apple's cofounder, chairman, and chief executive, Steve Jobs, to ascertain what people would want in their products [27]. This illustrates a particular CS behavior, *stimulates different perspectives (seek understanding)* of the environment, particularly potential customers.

Aqua-Aston Hospitality

Theresa van Greunen, Director of Public Relations and Promotions of Aqua-Aston Hospitality, one of Hawaii's largest hotel and resort operators (https://www.aquaaston.com/), responded graciously and quickly (the same day, 27 April 2018; maybe there are some updates she would like to offer) with a long list of relevant data, plus three attachments. Their main focus is protecting coral reefs, as well as human skin, through the development, distribution, and use of safe sunscreens by their millions of tourists. They also endeavor to eliminate single-use plastics and provide reusable, biodegradable materials and containers. Considerable detail about these laudable efforts was provided and is included below. Note the well-defined although limited focus of this organization, which helps to define the methodology of this study. However, they were unable to disclose detailed financial data, deeming it proprietary. Although this is quite understandable, such data would provide considerably more insight.

Aqua-Aston Hospitality began planning our "reef safe" public awareness initiative in 2016, after following the news about the global coral bleaching epidemic.

- We learned that coral bleaching is occurring especially in areas popular with tourists, in part, because of pollution — especially from sunscreen containing the chemicals oxybenzone and octinoxate.
- With more than 40 hotels and resorts throughout the state in Hawaii [also, in Orlando, FL, and Costa Rica], we accommodate 5.5 million guests each year. We recognized that we have a powerful opportunity — and an enormous responsibility — to help protect and preserve the natural environment that our guests come here to enjoy. [Profit and morality coincide.]
- While we understand there are many contributing factors to coral bleaching, raising awareness about the risks of some types of sunscreen is something we can easily do.
- We set out to 1) Raise public awareness about the dangers of some types of sunscreens on coral health, and that there are safer alternatives out there (so you can still protect your skin and the reef), and 2) Inspire a culture of sustainability among our partners in the tourism industry, in the hopes that our efforts would inspire an industry-wide approach towards raising public awareness and helping to preserve our natural environment.
- Our Corporate Social Responsibility program — called "Advocate with Aqua-Aston" — includes environmental stewardship.

- The Reef Safe campaign is the cornerstone of our environmental stewardship efforts, but is not the only aspect — we are also helping to eliminate single use plastics from our hotels by providing guests with reusable water bottles and canvas tote bags, reducing our waste and energy consumption, recycling, serving sustainable food in our restaurants, eliminating plastic straws, and using only biodegradable food containers. We encourage [One may wonder just what this entails.] all of our hotels and resorts to adopt the principles of Green Business.

- Our target audiences for our initiative include our local community here in Hawaii, our guests, key travel industry stakeholders, and the media — both in Hawaii, the mainland, and in key global markets where many of our visitors reside.

- Since the reef-safe campaign launched on Earth Day in April 2017, we have:
  o Provided the community, visitors and hotel guests with more than 40,000 samples of reef-safe sunscreen, and information on how to be reef-safe, at community events throughout Hawaii, as part of 'beach hits' throughout the islands, and at our hotels and resorts
  o Installed reef-safe sunscreen dispensers at multiple locations throughout Hawaii — including at the Waikiki Aquarium and our hotels and resorts
  o Encouraged sales of reef-safe sunscreen at our hotels and resorts, including at spas located on-site, and sundry shops located on-site
  o Launched a new amenity called the 'eco kit' to help our guests have a more sustainable stay, including a reusable shopping tote, a reusable water flask, and reef-safe sunscreen
  o Launched public awareness ads in Hawaii on six radio stations in Hawaii and on all three TV stations + Cable, generating
    12-million media impressions; To view the TV spot, please click on the following link: https://www.youtube.com/watch?v=sih13VfynFA
  o Generated more than 60-million media impressions with coverage about Aqua-Aston's efforts around this issue in national news outlets, including *The New York Times, the Los Angeles Times, San Francisco Chronicle, Travel + Leisure* and more
  o Provided financial support for nonprofits like the Waikiki Aquarium to bring in public speakers who are experts on corals and pollution

    o Providing financial support to for the Waikiki Aquarium's new coral exhibit and the coral propagation project

- Hosted three national media for a weeklong 'sustainability' themed FAM, including a 'deep dive' into what our community leaders are doing to establish a culture of sustainability here in Hawaii
- Hosted a Community Feast event in Feb 2018 with some of Hawaii's community leaders — designed to start a conversation on how we can all do our part to create a culture of sustainability and make positive impact in our community. Here is the list of some of the attendees:
  - o Ed Kenney, Mahina & Sun's/Town Hospitality
  - o Michael Wilson, Exhibit Designer 'Holo Moana' Bishop Museum
  - o Kaiulani Murphy, The Friends of Hōkūle'a
  - o Brian A. Guadagno, Founder/CEO, Raw Elements
  - o Alison Teal, Surfer/Activist Lisa Bishop, President, Friends of Hanauma Bay
  - o Ashley Watts, Owner, Local I'a Kahi Pacarro, Executive Director, Sustainable Coastline
  - o Chenoa Farnsworth, Managing Partner, Blue Startups
  - o Theresa van Greunen, Aqua-Aston Hospitality, Advocate with Aqua-Aston program, including Reef-Safe Initiatives
- Dr. Rich Pyle, Naturalist, Hawaii Biological Survey Staff, Bishop Museum Sponsored the Bishop Museum's Holo Moana exhibit which really encompasses what our efforts are all about, caring for the earth, caring for each other and for our community
- Encouraged our hotels and resorts to adopt the principals of Green Business and go through the process towards becoming 'green certified' through the Governor's Green Business program. So far, we have been recognized eight times.

In closing, this is a company-wide, long-term initiative for our company — not a short-term effort for Earth Day or Month, and we will roll out the program to all of our managed properties beyond Hawaii, in the Continental US and Costa Rica, by the end of 2018. [It would be nice to learn how this went.] I also want to share that it has become evident that there is a need to take the foundation that we have laid, to raise awareness that sunscreens containing ingredients that contribute to coral bleaching, to the next level. The next level is to raise awareness that, in addition to Raw Elements, there are *many* reef-safe sunscreen options available to purchase in Hawaii. We have heard feedback that people 'think' being reef safe means putting the health of your skin at risk, or that reef safe sunscreens are difficult to find when at the shop. So, in 2018 we will also expand our program by working with a roster of sunscreen producers that we can endorse as being reef-safe. The idea is to showcase the collection of brands, provide information on the many retail outlets where the consumer can purchase them, and continue our sampling distribution to emphasize that consumers have many reef-safe options.

Several elements of the CSE methodology of Chapter 2 (again, highlighted in italics just below) apply in this case. Aqua-Aston Hospitality made efforts to *understand the persistent problem* of coral reef damage and decided to mount two major efforts to combat further damage by helping to reduce harmful waste products, such as plastic containers, and developing good suntan lotions that banned harmful ingredients. The *mounting organizational efforts*, internally and externally, and *experimenting with users* in the field, as it were, led to public relations campaigns that helped *changing mindsights* and *stimulating self-organized collaborations* involving the public, public media, the tourist industry, and tourists.

Glenkinchie Distillery

On 11 May 2018, we toured this remarkable distillery in the East Lothian countryside, approximately an hour's drive outside of and southeast of Edinburgh, Scotland. A very knowledgeable guide gave us a private excursion throughout the place. The process of making scotch is quite well established, as explained in detail via museum-like exhibits and the personal walk through the plant. This type of Scottish malt whiskey requires only three ingredients: barley, yeast, and water. There are a few requirements to assure the final product is truly scotch, the main one being the liquid is cured for *at least* three years in an *oaken* cask.

The bottle we purchased at the end of the tour, for £22 (22 British Pounds), was a respectable 12 years old. Just before our guide tutored us on how to drink scotch properly, complete with a demonstration, (1) swirl it in the (small) glass provided and observe how it drifts downward on the inside, (2) appreciate the aroma by smelling the liquid with several wafts while keeping one's mouth open, and (3) gently sipping while swishing it around in the mouth before swallowing. It's a fine art!

Nothing is wasted or harms the environment! The whiskey at the intermediate stage consists of the "head," the "heart," and the "tail," the strongest, moderate, and weakest portions, respectively. The heart is passed on as the best brew, while the head and tail gets recycled and transformed into more heart. The water, steam, and other in-process vapors generated are also recycled. During the whole process, only 2% of the vapor is "lost to the angels."

All this is done along with the distillery's heroic efforts to protect the environment yet deliver world class refined spirits to Scotland and the world. Despite the significant financial, goodwill investments, and conscientiousness of their employees (that now number a lot fewer than in the olden days due to increased automation), Glenkinchie runs quite profitably and is a proud member of the parent company that oversees many other brands of liquor, e.g., Seagram's, B&B, Lagavulin, et al. We asked about Chivas Regal, but our guide immediately demurred: "That's a different company."

What aspects of the CSE methodology and principles might apply to this case? First, it is important to recognize that this situation is not very complex as CSs go. The distillery process was established gradually over many generations with much human input as to what worked well and what did not. Laudably, however, in contrast to many organizations that treat waste products as something to be expelled into the external environment, without regard to harmful effects, *Deciding* [the] *system boundary*, hopefully by consensus, is a fundamental step in the CSE methodology [22] and relates to an important principle, *utilize POET, define the CS boundary,* and *keep the big picture in mind* [26]. Glenkinchie did this well, showing sensible degrees of concern for protecting its surroundings.

Bill & Melinda Gates Foundation

This foundation is obviously very well known and quite respected; the Gates are contributing to humanitarian efforts big time, rightly sharing their wealth achieved by the phenomenal technological innovations introduced by Microsoft. Bill Gates has met with President Trump several times, and in March 2017 he at least briefly interested Mr. Trump in a universal flu vaccine. Bill is deeply committed to public health and effective responses to pandemics [28]. Their foundation is also pushing to help mitigate poverty in the US [29].

Recently, during the onset of the COVID-19 pandemic, reportedly (6 April 2020) the Microsoft billionaire Bill Gates says his foundation is funding the construction of a separate factory for each of seven coronavirus vaccine candidates (https://www.weforum.org/agenda/2020/04/bill-gates-7-potential-coronavirus-vaccines).

> Gates said the foundation would end up picking only one or two of the seven, meaning billions of dollars spent on manufacturing would be abandoned. He said that in a situation where the world faces the loss of trillions of dollars to the economy, wasting a few billion to help is worth it. … [He said his foundation] could mobilize faster than governments to fight the coronavirus outbreak. 'Because our foundation has such deep expertise in

infectious diseases, we've thought about the epidemic, we did fund some things to be more prepared, like a vaccine effort,' Gates said. 'Our early money can accelerate things.'

You might recognize from the above that Bill Gates is exercising several fundamental principles of CSE, *bring humility (acknowledge shortcoming and seek understanding), follow holism, (focus on the whole system rather than just the pieces),* and *achieve balance (shun optimality but improve overall capabilities).* We would be hard pressed to name a more laudable example of a private business leader who demonstrates his exceptional caring about the public interest by taking such actions.

Green Upward

In late 2017 Gabriella Jacobsen founded Green Upward, a company that makes eco-friendly reusable tote bags from 100% organic cotton, decorated with low-impact dyes and sewn in a fair-trade factory that employs Americans with disabilities. A percentage of the profits goes to Arcadia, an Alexandria, Virginia, organization that promotes sustainable food systems (https://greenupward.com/). She expressed sympathy with the cause of this chapter and offered several good ideas on the subject. (She sounds like a possible quotable source or advocate as a lead-in for a continued approach to other less responsive organizations.) For more, we encourage you to read the following excerpts from a relevant, motivating, and cogent article [30] she wrote.

> … I would suggest further research into sustainable business models. [Again, Gabriella might be approached for support as this research is continued.] I am aware of a couple companies who have tried to implement more sustainable practices and failed because they followed traditional business models that were not developed to handle sustainable initiatives. A couple recent business models I have been researching, which may be worth you looking into are: (1) Product as a service programs — see this Ellen Macarthur case study for example; (2) Material return/regeneration programs — where companies offer some incentive to their consumers to return the material at little to no cost and then the company creates another product from the fabric, etc.; or (3) Collecting and sorting programs that partner with municipalities, or other companies to effectively collect and sort end-of-life goods.
>
> As for leadership for positive change — I think it's critical to have sustainability engrained in the company culture and part of the mission statement. I think generally most folks want to make sustainable business choices but are not always encouraged to. I think developing a company culture that encourages sustainability can make a huge difference. This culture will

permeate into the decision making of middle and lower level management. I also believe transparency is key.

Shifting to becoming a more sustainable company is not easy as it requires the re-thinking of not just parts but whole systems within a company or manufacturer. Thus, transparency of how, when, and why the system is changing to more environmental practices is critical.

'Follow your mission, not your passion' — was a saying from one of my favorite design professors. I believe the next generation of designers and entrepreneurs has the responsibility to question what they make and focus on solutions that contribute real positive health, environmental, or cultural change — and that this change isn't reserved just for large companies.

I am two things: (1) Not very good at sitting still, and (2) an environmentally focused designer. The combination of these two traits led me to start a small design company called Green Upward in the year following my graduation from undergrad. I started off trying to live a more sustainable and zero waste lifestyle myself. The facts that kept bouncing around in my head were: 'It is now believed that there are 5.25 trillion pieces of plastic debris in the ocean. Shoppers worldwide are using approximately 500 billion single-use plastic bags per year. This translates to about a million bags every minute across the globe, or 150 bags a year for every person on earth. Over 100,000 marine creatures a year die from plastic entanglement and these are the ones found.' (Oceancrusaders.org)

I began to bring my own grocery tote bags, mason jars, and other containers with me to avoid my main source of plastic = grocery bags. I was standing in a Whole Foods, trying to collect bulk nuts, when a mason jar slipped out of my hand and shattered on the floor sending nut bits and glass shards everywhere. It was a Sunday afternoon grocery rush, and the Whole Foods members were not amused with my disruptive hippie-kid antics. I went online to look for a better solution and didn't find any durable, good-looking products. Furthermore, I learned I wasn't the only person struggling with braking mason jars in grocery stores. I realized it was time to put my design background to work.

I spent many months working on a prototype. My budget was next to zero, so I began by making bag prototypes with paper and other materials I found around my house to get a feel for the size and capability. Then I used scrap fabric and kept working to refine the design. I was adamant about limiting my materials and not using plastic in any form — even plastic thread. This quickly ruled out traditional closing mechanisms like clasps and zippers (even metal zippers are woven into plastic thread fabric). Finally, I worked with a seamstress to put together the complete pattern and prototype. I shipped this prototype to my manufacturer to copy and begin the production line. I spent countless hours researching materials and factories, looking for high quality goods and services that would match my cradle to cradle design philosophy. I was able to fulfill both, and now the bags can be cut up and composted at the end of their life and returned to the earth. Finally, I launched Green Upward's <u>Market</u> & Storage bags — produce and bulk food bags that sustainably collect, carry and store your food. Bags that also keep your food fresher for longer with their structured, breathable design. I launched a successful Kickstarter last August and now have been selling the bags through my online store and slowly building up the business.

With one simple design and a couple hundred bags sold, 300,000+ plastic bags have been saved from landfills and oceans — that's real impact. I love the initiatives I see in companies like REI, and Eileen Fisher — but you don't have to do a million in business to make a real positive change. Scale of course matters, but there are other ways to amplify your impact without compromising your business.

When you've created something with real impact — tell the story from your heart and start talking about it early. Consumers are oversaturated with flashy ads that now dominate Facebook pages and other social media sites. Don't create an ad, create a short story that highlights the features of what makes your idea great and what positive impacts it has on your consumer's life and the world. Begin talking about the 'why,' before you have all the details of the 'what' nailed down. A long launch time can be your company's best friend if used properly.

Create a relationship with the community you design for. Good companies solve problems, great companies redefine them. This means going back to the source of the issue and really speaking with individuals about their needs and pain-points. Find out which community of people you want to help. This could be young moms, eco-friendly folks, or stylish older men. Point is — you need to find the community of people you are serving and figure out how you can really help them. This community will guide your solutions and be the first buyers of your product or service.

You also need your own community to support you, whether that is friends, parents, neighbors, or more. Entrepreneurship is hard and you will need people to give you advice, proofread your materials, help you ship or whatever else comes your way. Also, consider looking into your local business resources. I recently signed up for free mentoring in Virginia from SCORE and received some great advice that way.

Finally, consider joining or forming a coalition with other companies that share elements of your supply chain or materials. Recently, I noticed a trend with sustainability focused companies: as they work towards more circular business models and circular product lifecycles; they create more partnerships with companies that complement their products are services. For example, Febreze, the air freshener company, now partners with Teracycle, a recycling company, to help their users properly recycle some of their products. I've also seen coalitions between companies within the same industry band together to increase their buying and negotiation power. You need to be big to change the industry, but you don't need to be big alone.

As I continue to push Green Upward forward in the coming year, I will continue to strengthen my community relationships as well as look to expand them in my industry. Every day I see more and more individuals looking to make positive environmental changes through business and design and that thrills me. I hope as a collective we revolutionize the way people choose and buy their goods and services, for our benefit, and for the benefit of generations to come.

Talk about leadership! Here's a woman who is into encouraging others to do the right things without any up-front expectations or promises of financial compensation.

Here are a few of the CSE principles we think Gabriella has applied, *nurture discussions (listen to others and reward information sharing), pursue opportunities (take informed risks by pursuing alternative solutions)*, and *foster trust(brave personal vulnerability in gaining help from others)*. The world is becoming a little better place because of her efforts.

Hurtigruten Foundation

The Hurtigruten cruise lines organization, especially the Hurtigruten Foundation, https://www.hurtigruten.com/, has several humanitarian outreach efforts. To name a few: stimulating education/schools via The Association of Greenlandic Children; the preserving of penguin and other natural habitats; making smaller environmental footprints; campaigns aimed at the reduction of plastic waste; and the nurturing of arctic regions championed by Lewis Pugh, a long-distance swimmer who incredibly publicizes this mission by swimming in frigid waters.

Postulating desirable outcome spaces and *proposing specific interventions* are two aspects of the CSE methodology that apply here, in addition to most of those already exhibited by Aqua-Aston Hospitality. The vision that usually precedes the definition of wanted outcomes is mainly the responsibility of the principal leader of the effort. The outcome space does not contain solutions but is used to test possible solutions to be assured they are consistent with desirability. Outcome spaces are analogous to what headlights illuminate in driving down road a road at night; the beams are wide enough to present promising opportunities as well as warnings against hazards, and this cogent view is continually adjusted as one progresses. Occasionally, based on what is observed, actions are taken, i.e., specific interventions, to modify the trip itinerary.

Negative Examples

Now we mention a couple of organizations that reflect at least partially negative postures and/or accomplishments.

Equifax

This company notoriously exposed personal information, including Social Security numbers, possibly 143 million, of their subscribers/users.

We tried to query them about positive humanitarian accomplishments in an attempt to balance their "bad press." However, although their Customer Care Team initially said they would work diligently to consider our case, shortly thereafter they were "pleased" to close it without responding in any fashion to the specifics of our request. How can one not feel a little bit suspicious or even somewhat angry about that response?

Facebook

Mark Zuckerberg is notorious for stealing the Facebook's initial social networking ideas from his colleagues at Harvard after being asked by them to help develop the feasible implementation technology. Although he was able to do so, he seemingly and unfairly locked them out of the action. In the ensuing lawsuits, Zuckerberg ultimately bought them off for relatively paltry sum of several million dollars.

As has become abundantly clear from a fairly recent scandal, exposing up to 87 million users' private information, Facebook primarily cares about making tons of money, regardless of often the nefarious nature of applications of this medium, including bogus or provably false information by Russian-backed operatives, let alone mindless promulgation or repetition by normal users and unexpected consequences to innocent and unsuspecting users. We doubt whether Facebook will change its ways significantly, especially if Zuckerberg remains in charge.

Zuckerberg basically ignored most of the risks in pursuing the Facebook opportunities of creating wealth by providing a popular social platform for public use. The most glaring risks included the misuses of the media and the loss of privacy. Most users pursued the opportunity of connecting socially, also without considering the downsides. Both the developers and the users should have balanced the opportunities and risks because both aspects are important.

Facebook's clear self-interest at the expense of truth, fact checking, and reasonable profit making, as well as Zuckerberg's stalwart defense of its operating procedures, continues to be controversial (https://www.cnn.com/2020/01/29/tech/facebook-earnings/index.html). It will be interesting to see what develops with Facebook while other organizations move forward with their more humanitarian efforts.

Balancing opportunities and risks is the principal aspect of the CSs methodology that applies here. In a healthy CS, it's all about pursuing opportunities with informed risks. In traditional systems engineering, there is much more focus on risks and trying to get back on the originally conceived track when things seem to go astray. However, in complex systems that continually evolve, more attention should be devoted to potential benefits of opportunities that are presented or conjured up. Nevertheless, such opportunities should be explored keeping possible downside risks in mind.

ROLE-MODEL EXAMPLES OF HUMANITARIAN INVESTMENTS

Since it has been difficult to get relevant financial data from the above survey efforts, here are some articles, websites, and statistics related to what several organizations are spending on humanitarian efforts.

It is understandable that economic trends affect giving, in that companies are more charitable in good times than in bad. Also worthy of note are consumers' and employees' perceptions of businesses with corporate philanthropic programs.

Notable Articles

One article [31] excerpted just below, contains good financial data on (1) average and total charitable cash and in-kind giving by British industry and (2) proportions of companies and amounts given to various causes.

> There is a very long tradition of businesses donating money, goods or staff time to charitable causes, all of which falls under the umbrella of corporate philanthropy. But unlike an individual's decision to make a donation to a Children in Need appeal or support the Ice Bucket Challenge to do their bit and have a warm inner glow, the motivation for a company to make a donation in whatever form it may take is considerably more complex.
>
> In the past, many companies have donated to charities because they wanted to give something back and 'do good,' says Klara Kozlov, head of corporate clients at the Charities Aid Foundation. However, there is a now a growing awareness that philanthropy can be a powerful way of tackling issues that affect their business operations, as well as society more broadly. ...
> That has led to a growing number of partnerships between corporates and charities or non-governmental organizations. ...

A prime example of this trend can be found in the Vodafone Foundation, which was set up in 1991 and spends about £45 million annually across 27 countries. Andrew Dunnett, its director, says the philosophy has changed from 'we've done well, we should do some good' that it had at the start to 'how to do good as part of doing well in business.'

'We've moved away from the cheque-book charity that has symbolised corporate giving in the past. We're giving away the same amount of money, but there is much more that we can do with our people, our technology and combining that with our charitable giving to make a difference in the communities in which we operate,' he says. ...

'When people see the power of connecting our technology to the giving and using our skills, rather than just giving, it makes a huge difference in people's minds,' he adds. ...

Research into organisational behaviour has found the relationship employees have with their organisation – how it makes them feel and what opportunities it offers for personal growth – is becoming just as important as their remuneration, according to Ms. Kozlov.

'There used to be a divide between who you are in your personal life and your professional life, but that is changing and people are applying the same profile to their professional life as their personal life. They need to feel authentic in the workplace and, therefore, the values of their organisation become much more important,' she says. ... the Charities Aid Foundation finding that 51% of British adults would be more likely to buy a product or use a service from a company that donates to charitable causes ...

Some companies are more willing to shout about their philanthropic activities than others, even going as far as featuring it in advertising or social media campaigns. No matter how a company decides to go about its philanthropy, Ms. Kozlov believes the overriding factor for an organisation is being genuine. 'The public very quickly detects when something isn't authentic ... a company can demonstrate its social purpose as long as it feels genuine, and not being used as a sales and marketing tool,' she says.

Here are a couple of quotes from another article [32] that suggest that people's experience with a company's products is enhanced if they know the organization supports "good" causes. This constitutes the "halo" effect of being aligned with worthy activities, at least in public perception, if not fact.

Does wine taste better if you know the vintner donates to a worthy charity? Will a teeth whitener make your pearly whites look even whiter if the manufacturer funds child relief efforts? The answer, according to new research from the Kellogg School, is yes.

Many companies engage in corporate social responsibility at least partly as a marketing effort – a way to enhance the reputation of a company's brand. But Alexander Chernev, a professor of marketing at the Kellogg School of Management, and Sean Blair, at Georgetown University, show that knowing that a company has behaved ethically can cause customers to perceive that company's products as performing better. They call this effect a 'benevolent halo.' This is a different story than just saying, 'People like the company more,' says Chernev. 'The increase in positive perception is not based on advertising. Consumers actually experience the product in a different way.'

An excellent article [33] from the Harvard Business review discusses the synergistic ideal of achieving both corporate profits and social impact, combining business with psychology.

> ... Corporations can use their charitable efforts to improve their *competitive context* — the quality of the business environment in the location or locations where they operate. Using philanthropy to enhance context brings social and economic goals into alignment and improves a company's long-term business prospects .... In addition, addressing context enables a company not only to give money but also to leverage its capabilities and relationships in support of charitable causes. That produces social benefits far exceeding those provided by individual donors, foundations, or even governments. ...
>
> Should corporations engage in philanthropy at all? The economist Milton Friedman laid down the gauntlet decades ago, arguing in a 1970 *New York Times Magazine* article that the only 'social responsibility of business' is to 'increase its profits.' 'The corporation,' he wrote in his book *Capitalism and Freedom*, 'is an instrument of the stockholders who own it. If the corporation makes a contribution, it prevents the individual stockholder from himself deciding how he should dispose of his funds.' If charitable contributions are to be made, Friedman concluded, they should be made by individual stockholders — or, by extension, individual employees — and not by the corporation.
>
> The way most corporate philanthropy is practiced today, Friedman is right. ...
>
> But does Friedman's argument always hold? Underlying it are two implicit assumptions. The first is that social and economic objectives are separate and distinct, so that a corporation's social spending comes at the expense of its economic results. The second is the assumption that corporations, when they address social objectives, provide no greater benefit than is provided by individual donors. These assumptions hold true when corporate contributions are unfocused and piecemeal, as is typically the case today. But there is another, more truly strategic way to think about philanthropy. Corporations can use their charitable efforts to improve their *competitive context* of the quality of the business environment in the location or locations where they operate. Using philanthropy to enhance context brings social and economic goals into alignment and improves a company's long-term business prospects – thus contradicting Friedman's first assumption. In addition, addressing context enables a company not only to give money but also to leverage its capabilities and relationships in support of charitable causes. That produces

social benefits far exceeding those provided by individual donors, foundations, or even governments. Context-focused giving thus contradicts Friedman's second assumption as well. ...

That does not mean that every corporate expenditure will bring a social benefit or that every social benefit will improve competitiveness. Most corporate expenditures produce benefits only for the business, and charitable contributions unrelated to the business generate only social benefits. It is only where corporate expenditures produce simultaneous social and economic gains that corporate philanthropy and shareholder interests converge, as illustrated in the exhibit 'A Convergence of Interests.' The highlighted area shows where corporate philanthropy has an important influence on a company's competitive context. It is here that philanthropy is truly strategic. ...

Philanthropy can often be the most cost-effective way for a company to improve its competitive context, enabling companies to leverage the efforts and infrastructure of nonprofits and other institutions. ...

There is no inherent contradiction between improving competitive context and making a sincere commitment to bettering society.

Here's an author [34] who suggests four ways to make charitable efforts work well for organizations. He explains each of his points in detail within this citation.

Modern society gives some great rewards to entrepreneurs who find what people need and want, and provide it. This exchange is huge part to the free market philosophy that has led to much prosperity (although unfortunately not for everyone). Successful businesspeople are well rewarded for their ability to provide what society wants. Sometimes these people make for good philanthropists, even if many are still stingy with their wealth.

Charitable acts are performed without the expectation of direct financial gain, but they certainly are not without their own rewards. Here are four of the major ways that successful businesspeople and even you can benefit by giving to charitable causes.

1. Building respect and a good reputation in the community.
2. Making your community a better place to live.
3. Employees respect leaders who do good.
4. Connections and networking.

This article [35] provides detailed financial data on contributions of many companies, as well as some indications of the nature of their efforts.

By surveying the top 150 companies in the Fortune 500 and collecting data from public documents filed with the IRS and SEC, *The Chronicle of Philanthropy* has published a list of the most charitable public companies, which can be viewed here. With help from the *Chronicle, Fortune* has identified the top 20 most generous companies, as measured by cash contributions. The dollar amounts cited below were independently verified by *Fortune*. In total, the 20 most generous companies donated $3.5 billion in cash in 2015.

Notable Websites

Attempts to contact a person at Coca-Cola [36] were unsuccessful. But here is something from its website (https://www.coca-colacompany.com/our-company/the-coca-cola-foundation).

Since our inception in 1984, The Coca-Cola Foundation has given back more than $820 million to enhance the sustainability of local communities worldwide.

The Coca-Cola Foundation is our Company's primary international philanthropic arm. The Foundation was established in the US as a registered 501(c)(3) charitable organization. Foundations grants are awarded throughout the year based on our priorities, tax requirements, legal compliance and approval by the Foundation's Board of Directors.

All requests for community support in the form of grants or sponsorships must be submitted through our online application system.

Overview: In 1984, Roberto Goizueta, then Chairman and CEO of The Coca-Cola Company, established The Coca-Cola Foundation. Over the past three decades, The Foundation has grown from a local foundation into a global philanthropic organization.

The Coca-Cola Company is committed to giving back 1% of its prior year's operating income annually. This commitment is made through The Coca-Cola Foundation and company donations. In 2015, The Coca-Cola Company and The Coca-Cola Foundation gave back more than $117 million to directly benefit nearly 300 organizations across more than 70 countries and territories.

Since its inception, the Foundation has supported learning inside and outside the classroom. However, addressing critical community challenges and opportunities is an evolving process. In 2007, the Foundation broadened its support to include global water stewardship programs, fitness and nutrition efforts and community recycling programs. Today, our strategies align with the Company's Sustainability platform and include women's empowerment and entrepreneurship.

Priority Areas: Women: economic empowerment and entrepreneurship

- Water: access to clean water, water conservation and recycling
- Well-Being: education, youth development and other community and civic initiatives

In addition, the Foundation supports many local community programs such as arts and culture, community and economic development programs in the

United States, as well as HIV/AIDS prevention and awareness programs in Africa and Latin America.

Our community commitment is shared across The Coca-Cola system. When natural disasters strike, The Coca-Cola Foundation and the entire Coca-Cola system respond to offer emergency relief.

Through the Coca-Cola Matching Gifts Program, eligible employees make personal contributions to qualified organizations and The Coca-Cola Foundation matches those contributions on a 2-for-1 basis.

Download a complete list of 2017 Foundation grants and corporate donations.

A similar website from [37] contains the following.

The Starbucks Foundation was created as part of our commitment to strengthen communities.

We started in 1997 by funding literacy programs in the United States and Canada. Today we're supporting communities around the globe.

The Starbucks Foundation gave $6.9 million in 2015, making 128 grants to nonprofit organizations. Grants included $3 million for Starbucks Opportunity for Youth Grants and $1.5 million in social development grants.

In 2015 Starbucks Corporation gave $29 million in cash, including $14 million to the Starbucks Foundation. Corporate giving included funding for community-building programs — including the Global Fund through our partnership with (RED)™ and other efforts — and $29.3 million in in-kind contributions.

Opportunity for Youth: The Starbucks Foundation believes in providing young people, ages 16 to 24 years old, with pathways to opportunity by investing in programs that equip young people with the skills required for the changing global economy.

Community Service: The Starbucks Foundation also supports our partners' (employees) engagement in their local community through Partner Match and Community Service Grants. These programs provide matching grants to nonprofits where our partners made personal monetary and time contributions. Coming together in service represents a fundamental act of citizenship for individuals, businesses and community members to create a stronger, more cohesive society.

Supporting Coffee, Tea and Cocoa Communities: Our commitment to communities extends beyond our stores to include the regions that supply our coffee, tea and cocoa. Starbucks invests in programs designed to strengthen local economic and social development. We work collaboratively with non-governmental organizations that have experience and expertise in working with farming communities in the countries where coffee, and other agricultural products are raised. Projects include improving access to education and agricultural training, microfinance and microcredit services, improving biodiversity conservation, and increasing levels of health, nutrition and water sanitation.

Access to Clean Water: Ethos Water began as a social venture startup with the goal of providing people in developing countries with access to clean water. For every bottle of Ethos® water sold in the United States, 5 cents is directed to the Ethos© Water Fund to help finance water programs around the world. Since 2005 $13.8 million has been granted through the Ethos Water Fund, benefitting more than 500,000 people around the world.

Relevant Statistics

Here are some other statistics that might be of interest.

Apple: Apple CEO Tim Cook donates $100 million to charity. Apple's CEO announces that he spent $100M of Apple's money on charitable giving — something Steve Jobs would not have done. 2 February 2012. (https://www.huffingtonpost.com/2012/02/03/apple-charity-donation_n_1253185.html)

Walmart: Overall, Walmart and the Walmart Foundation's total global contributions of $1.08B in the last fiscal year include: US giving of $1B in cash and in-kind gifts, up from $872.7M last year. 22 April 2013. (https://news.walmart.com/news-archive/2013/04/22/walmart-giving-in-last-fiscal-year-exceeds-1-billion-for-the-first-time)

Google: Google charitable donations set record. San Francisco – Google's third annual Global Giving Week netted $24M, double what it raised last year, as employees spread the wealth. 20 December 2016. (https://www.usatoday.com/story/tech/news/2016/12/20/google-charitable-donations-set-record/95636922/)

Catholic Charities: In 2010, Catholic Charities USA reported expenditures of between $4.2B and $4.4B, according to the Chronicle of Philanthropy, which publishes an annual list of the 400 biggest charities in the United States, ranked by the amount of donations they receive. 19 March 2013. (http://www.politifact.com/truth-o-meter/statements/2013/mar/19/frank-keating/does-catholic-church-provide-half-social-services-/)

WHAT MORE MIGHT BE ADVOCATED

Laurence D. Fink is founder and chief executive of BlackRock, an influential investment firm. According to an article [38] in *The New York Times*, Mr. Fink has applied leverage (via a letter to CEOs) advocating increased humanitarian efforts, i.e., taking on more social responsibility, within the world's largest public companies by threatening to withdraw support otherwise.

... [C]ompanies need to do more than make profits — they need to contribute to society as well if they want to receive the support of BlackRock. Mr. Fink has the clout to make this kind of demand: His firm manages more than $6 trillion in investments through 401(k) plans, exchange-traded funds and mutual funds, making it the largest investor in the world, and he has an outsize influence on whether directors are voted on and off boards.

"Society is demanding that companies, both public and private, serve a social purpose," he wrote in a draft of the letter that was shared with me. "To prosper over time, every company must not only deliver financial performance, but also show how it makes a positive contribution to society." ...

Despite Mr. Fink's insistence that companies benefit society, it's worth noting he's not playing down the importance of profits and, while it's a subtle point, he believes that having social purpose is inextricably linked to a company's ability to maintain its profits. ...

Maybe this will catch on! Mr. Fink's action suggests that other influential leaders might apply similar pressures to those in authority within other domains.

This brings to mind the possibility of a two-edged sword, begging the question as to whether Fink would support a very worthy global cause if it actually ran counter to his firm's money-making talents, thereby not only decreasing his income, most likely, but possibly depleting the funds necessary to do this major incentivizing. It is tricky whenever the subjective choice of what's important is left mainly to the upper 1%, realistic though that may seem to be. (Could this be considered a problem with capitalism?)

Is there a possibility, in such cases, for an objective board, working as volunteers and possibly anonymously, to research causes and make suggestions? That might be an omnipresent "foundation" type thing, partly justified by separating themselves from the tendency to think of bottom line as not only equal in worthiness with an altruistic cause but far preceding or obscuring it? This idea is expanded upon in the next section.

CONSIDER CREATING AN INTERNAL THINK (AND DO) TANK

Here are a few suggestions on forming a special internal change management entity and starting its operation on productive pathways toward objectives more global than typically considered by many organizations.

Defining a Think and Do Tank

This think tank idea was inspired by some passages in Madeleine Albright's recent book [39].

> [Post World War II], the modern conception [of "think tank"] came into vogue: a research organization dedicated to public policy. (p. 163)
> There is a critical difference between a think tank that tries to be balanced, checks its facts, and recruits scholars who have a range of perspectives and one whose overriding purpose is to make the case for a pre-existing point of view. This distinction, which should be obvious, is becoming increasingly blurred as partisans define and peddle their own versions of reality and, in the fervor of competition, try to undercut the whole notion of disinterested research. (p. 168)

The idea here is for any organization, particularly companies, to consider encouraging the formation of a sort or type of internal think tank, not necessarily a research group or suborganization, but rather a body of volunteers composed of leaders, technical staff, technicians, office workers, etc., that commit some of their time to identifying and developing the type of good causes espoused in this chapter. Albright further expounds on the worthiness of this type of cause.

> My best moments in business are those that most clearly inform and complement other aspects of my life. That is when the projects we work on have tangible social benefits. ... Ideally [an] enterprise [or complex system, system of systems, system, or organization] would always do well by doing good, but I have yet to find anyone who thinks that as a business plan, altruism is enough. (p. 201) ... [I]ntegrating ethical and civic-minded behavior into a corporation's culture is both possible and smart. This isn't just a matter of public relations. Employees work more diligently and stay longer with firms that are good local citizens and whose priorities they respect. [They] want to be proud of what [they] do. (p. 202)

The trick is for those in charge of any organization, the board of directors, the chief executive and other corporate officers, division and department heads, group leaders, or whomever, to allocate a significant expenditure of company resources toward this endeavor and to encourage the formation, operation, publication, and rewarding of the internal think tank. Clearly, this is not just a group of thinkers; they are expected to be doers, as well!

Suggestion as to How to Begin

I had an inspirational dream the night of 9–10 April 2020 where we tried to sell an off-the-cuff outlined procedure for complex change management to an inside group of colleagues plus the leader in charge. Evidently, the pitch was so compelling that everyone got excited and all were eager to try it out. It went something like this.

To encourage and stimulate a laudable group effort to suggest a purpose whose accomplishments might make a significant difference, each person should separately create an abbreviated (hopefully on one-page but no more than two-pages) input including:

- Today's Date:
- Member Name:
- Member e-mail address:
- Member Telephone Number(s), home, cell (mobile):
- Core, Basic, or Fundamental Idea:
- Applicability Domain(s), e.g., research, development, improvement, etc.:
- Potential Areas of Application(s):
- Possible Collaborators, e.g., external individuals or organizations:
- Desired Outcome Space:
- Laudable Goals:
- Opportunities and Downside (Informed) Risks:
- Potential Exciting Venn Diagram Overlaps with Other Inputs:

The leader would then collect these inputs and see that copies were made for everyone present. While that was being done, each contributor could also document his or her core idea on a yellow sticker; these would all be pasted on the wall for perusal by the group. After a suitable but limited time, the group would reassemble and peruse everyone's suggestions while each contributor presented his or her input and answered questions.

At this point the objective would be to attempt reaching a consensus on which suggestions to pursue and in which order of priority, perhaps. We suggest that no more than three be selected, with the others filed away for potential future use. Teams would be chosen to pursue the three current "winners" that would be developed in parallel. Participants could be part of more than one team if they so desired.

A tentative plan for next steps, including a rough schedule and dates for future progress report meetings, would be proposed collectively.

Note that all this is merely a suggested a way to begin. Of course, additional planning and re-planning would be required. One very important aspect to consider is contingencies. Early on in this effort, the group should define a fairly specific procedure to follow (religiously) when unexpected events occur, as surely they will with complex systems.

Suggested Example Endeavors

Here we attempt to motivate *social responsibility* actions in just two important realms of current interest, surviving pandemics and becoming better informed.

COVID-19

Some of the areas of potential effort are vaccine development, contagion and anti-body testing, tracking of exposed individuals, provision of protective gear, application of disinfectants, personal cleansing, wearing of masks and gloves, and social distancing. We suggest that the first three of these are most worthy and in greater need of assistance. The fourth area, although still exhibiting shortages, is being dealt with pretty well, but see [40] for a fertile discussion of this issue. The rest of these areas have been adequately publicized and are being, or should be, followed by caring individuals using common sense.

There are likely several things that almost any credible organization with a sound methodology could do to accelerate vaccine development, testing, and tracking. How about mounting well-planned campaigns to

- *Learn more* (through literature or media searches to enhance ongoing efforts) about the
  - possible applicability of existing drugs or their modifications, then *organize* and *report these results* to key researchers, possibly to increase their knowledge
  - *ongoing or planned experimental trials* and then work toward *finding* and *enlisting more volunteers* to serve as "guinea pigs"
- *Collect* and *organize* (e.g., in spreadsheets using logical and understandable formats) *vaccine development* data for
  - *transmission to knowledgeable authorities* for their consideration and potential use
  - *publication* in the press, periodicals (e.g., *The Week*) news shows, or other social media
- *Become aware* of potentially *useful information* being *blocked* from release by the Trump administration, and

- o *send* summaries to *objective/responsible media* outlets like *The Rachel Maddow Show* (she has promised to make that data public)

- Put apparently disconnected but potentially related researchers in touch with each other for
  - o their *mutual benefit*
  - o *stimulating further progress* toward an effective vaccine

- Contact testers and offer help in organizing further testing in lacking areas by
  - o *locate and educate untested people*, especially those at greater risk, about testing
  - o safely *bringing willing people to test sites* and returning them home
  - o *offer volunteers* to be *trained* as *testers* (this frees first responders to return to their primary responsibilities instead of being testers; e.g., Sean Penn is helping in this way)
  - o *Contribute to* the *costs of testing*

- Consider designing or distributing an effective and pervasive way of tracking exposed people
  - o using *existing mobile phone* or other applicable technologies
  - o recovering and *distributing tracking data* for action while protecting privacy

- *Create* and *assist* in sign up *petitions* for mounting what might be considered "good" causes — or even legislation — related to or impacting the repercussions of COVID-19
- *Reward helpers* battling virus with
  - o *financial* assistance
  - o *commendations* on *public* or *social media*

Obviously, you might be able to participate in a brainstorm to critique, improve, and/or add to this rather crude and incomplete list.

Getting to the Truth

Some things have already been said about this topic near the end of Chapter 2 and excesses of social media subsection near the beginning of this chapter.

We think President Trump and his administration have created a very contentious political climate in the US that largely ignores facts by continually promulgating misstatements of ("alternative") facts, frequent untruths, or outright lies, most often without any offered supporting information to justify the claims. For example, in May 2020, our president, in contrast to praising China earlier for its handling of the virus problem, was trying to shift all blame to that country for delays in preparing for the COVID-19 pandemic [41]. This is a prime characteristic of autocrats and behavior that is dangerous to the survival of democracy that is founded on the populace having access to and knowing the truth. What might a typical organization do in this regard?

One of the first actions that may come to mind is mounting a massive write-in campaign addressed to prominent (and certainly local) members of the House of Representatives and the Senate to highlight and summarize the problems and suggest potential pathways toward improvement. Unfortunately, this might be fruitless considering the extreme level of partisanship that often seems to pervade this institution. But some members might be persuasively swayed by their local constituents if they see that their re-election is in jeopardy. Financial contributions, especially those that outweigh those from lobbyists, might be even more powerful in stimulating their latent patriotism, perhaps.

The broadcast media could become another worthy target for our admonitions. These organizations are driven by high ratings and the airing of lucrative commercials based upon the self-interests of private enterprise. Their purpose seems to be entertainment, not education, of the public. Far too much airtime is devoted to repetition of "breaking news" (when nothing really new is offered), Trump's lies (are repeated incessantly [except for Rachel Maddow, who generally avoids this practice of amplification as being detrimental to public edification and who pays more attention to what Trump does rather than what he says {except for what she aired in her 11 May 2020 show, for example}]), and inane commercials (why would anyone buy these products based on the ads?). Apparently, a large portion of the public has rather low standards for what their viewing time is worth. To them, most of what is offered is more valuable than reading a good book, for example. How can that attitude be sustained if we are to preserve our democracy?

Social, professional, and media sharing networks, e.g., Facebook, Twitter, Linked-In, ResearchGate, Instagram, Snapchat, YouTube, etc., have greatly expanded our access to current (much) data, (often) information, (sometimes) understanding, and (more rarely) wisdom. These have the coronavirus advantage of making physical distancing more tenable, for sure, but are these networks really that conducive to reaping the benefits of in-person interactions? Our younger people, for instance, are becoming increasingly distant from genuine human contact and self-absorbed with their largely hand-held devices. Maybe there are some promising ways of developing trusted applications that would more accurately rate the degree of truths versus untruths of what is transmitted and received.

CONCLUSION

We have tried to make a credible case for devoting more organizational resources toward the public good instead of concentrating just on maximizing profits. If and when this is achieved, those involved in leading such efforts and making them happen should feel better about their work, and the public will thank them for it, hopefully by seeking more of the organization's products or services and paying for them.

But what might it mean to "feel better," specifically and tangibly? We submit that such contributors will be able to begin most every working day with enthusiasm in anticipation of furthering progress toward agreed-to goals in a collectively established, desired outcome space and conclude most every working day with at least a mental accounting of steps taken that have a good chance of success. Thus, one should be able to sleep relatively contentedly most every night while knowing, however, that good feelings should be tempered by the understanding that influencing complex systems in truly positive directions can be difficult and that patience as well as some humility is required to maintain sanity. In short, hopefully one feels the world will or at least might become better off through this type effort.

The basic idea of a desirable outcome space for almost any organization is to combine improved profitability with the moral leadership necessary for moving toward greater humanitarian efforts. This notion is depicted qualitatively in Figure 3.1 for a new organization. The initial condition is zero profit (from *social responsibilities* contributions) and no (such) humanitarian contributions. The first objective is to make some money, hopefully while contributing a modicum of social benefit, as shown incrementally by the start of the "wiggly" pathway. As the organization grows in the desired direction, more or less emphasis is given to profitability or humanitarian efforts depending on the current situation, perhaps affected by the local and/or global economies. Pre-planned procedures should be in place to guard against going beyond the agreed-to limits in either direction, which could lead to imbalances and possibly dire consequences that might cause the demise of the organization.

RECOMMENDATIONS

Future work on this topic could entail case and business model studies to further test the hypotheses espoused here. This can be difficult, especially

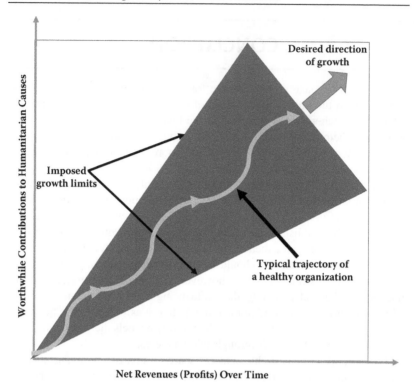

FIGURE 3.1   Sample Operational Trajectory.

because most organizations are reluctant to share proprietary methods and internal financial data, even though some of this sharing would be beneficial to all and not threaten their operations.

Any follow-up survey should consider asking how government regulations affect the business. Specifically, it would be interesting to gauge the extent to which successful humanitarian efforts ease the path to greater profitability, as well, perhaps because of less government oversight or interference.

ACKNOWLEDGMENTS

Thanks to Ms. Hilary Basile for providing several excellent examples of corporate/organizational humanitarian efforts; to Chad Walker for suggesting his former employer, AMD, as an exemplar; to Theresa van Greunen and Gabriella Jacobsen, especially, for their timely, positive, and generous survey responses; and to Nadia Creamer for her detailed and thorough reviews and astute comments.

REFERENCES

1. Social Responsibility (2018) *Wikipedia, The Free Encyclopedia.* https://en.wikipedia.org/wiki/Social_responsibility.
2. The Week (2020) "Canada: Is gun ban too much or too little?" *The Week.* 15 May 2020. p. 17.
3. The Week (March 2018) "Our other example for America." *The Week.* 9 March 2018. p. 15.
4. Born, Dana H. & Goldstein, Josh A. (2018) "How business leaders can be moral leaders." Boston Globe. 15 March 2018. https://www.bostonglobe.com/opinion/letters/2018/03/21/troubled-times-sos-sent-corporate-world/cnVcASpTKR63rP5pYy1jAM/story.html.
5. "Bullying, Cyberbullying, & Suicide Statistics." https://meganmeierfoundation.org/statistics.
6. Zdanow, C., and Wright, B. (2012) "The Representation of Self Injury and Suicide on Emo Social Networking Groups." African Sociological Review. Vol. 16 No. 2 (2012). https://www.ajol.info/index.php/asr/article/view/87564.
7. Orwell, George (1949). *1984.* New York: Harcourt, Inc.
8. Voltaire (1765) "Questions sur les miracles." essay.
9. The Week (April 2018) Social media: Why is it so hard to quit? *The Week.* 13 April 2018. p. 18.
10. White, B. E. (2012) "Let's Do Better in Limiting Material Growth to Conserve Our Earth's Resources." Conference on Systems Engineering Research (CSER). St. Louis, MO. 19–22 March 2012.
11. White, B. E. (2013). "Applying Complex Systems Engineering in Balancing Our Earth's Population and Natural Resources." *7thInternational Conference for Systems Engineering of the Israeli Society for Systems Engineering* (INCOSE_IL). Herzlia, Israel. 4–5 March 2013.
12. White, B. E. (2019) "Engineering One's Quality of Life as an SoS." 14th Annual System of Systems Engineering (SoSE) Conference 2016. Anchorage, Alaska. 19–22 May 2019.
13. Lister, N-M. (2008). Bridging Science and Values: "The Challenge of Biodiversity Conservation." In Waltner-Toews, D., Kay, J.J., and Lister, N-M.E. *The Ecosystem Approach: Complexity, Uncertainty, And Managing for Sustainability.* New Columbia University Press: New York. pp. 83–107.
14. The Week (2020) "The world at a glance… – Wellington, New Zealand." *The Week.* 15 May 2020. p. 9.

15. White, B.E. (2017). "Fathoming the Future of Artificially Intelligent Robots." *International Journal of Design & Nature and Ecodynamics*. Papers from Complex Systems Conference. New Forest, UK. 23-25 May 2017. Vol. 13, No. 1. pp. 1–15.

16. Public Citizen (2017). Mass mailing material. 1600 20th Street, NW, Washington, D.C. 20009. www.citizen.org.

17. White, B. E., and Gandhi, S. J. (2013) "The Case for Online College Education——a work in progress." American Society for Engineering Education (ASEE) Annual Conference. Atlanta, GA. 23–26 June 2013.

18. Gorod, A., White, B.E., Ireland, V., Gandhi, S.J., & Sauser, B.J. (2015) *Case Studies in System of Systems, Enterprise Systems, and Complex Systems Engineering*. Boca Raton: CRC Press, Taylor & Francis Group.

19. Waltner-Toews, D., Kay, J. J., and Lister, N-M. E. (2008) *The Ecosystem Approach: Complexity, Uncertainty, and Managing for Sustainability*. New York: Columbia University Press.

20. Berkes, F., & Davidson-Hunt, I. (2008). "The Cultural Basis for an Ecosystem Approach: Sharing Across Systems of Knowledge." In Waltner-Toews, D., Kay, J.J., and Lister, N-M.E. *The Ecosystem Approach: Complexity, Uncertainty, and Managing for Sustainability*. New York: New Columbia University Press. pp. 109–124.

21. Almond, Steve (2018) *Bad Stories: What the Hell Just Happened to Our Country?* Pasadena: Red Hen Press.

22. White, B.E. (2016) A Complex Adaptive Systems Engineering (CASE) Methodology: The Ten-Year Update. *IEEE Systems Conference*, Orlando, FL. 18–21 April 2016.

23. Lee, Michael Y., & Edmondson, Amy C. (2017) Self-Managing Organizations: Exploring the Limits of Less-Hierarchical Organizing. *Research in Organizational Behavior*. January 2017. DOI: 10.1016/j.riob.2017.10.002.

24. White, B.E. (2015) On Leadership in the Complex Adaptive Systems Engineering of Enterprise Transformation. *Journal of Enterprise Transformation*. Vol. 3, pp. 192–217. 11 September 2015, Supplementary Material (Appendices) http://www.tandfonline.com/doi/suppl/10.1080/19488289.2015.1056450; ISSN: 1948-8289 (Print) 1948-8297 (Online) Journal homepage: http://www.tandfonline.com/loi/ujet20; http://dx.doi.org/10.1080/19488289.2015.1056450.

25. Ably (2018) http://filium.com/.

26. White, B. E. (2016) "Complex Systems: How to Recognize Them and Engineer Them." Tutorial/Workshop. Tuesday, 14 June 2016. Krona – Kongsberg Kunnskap og kulturpark. Home of Buskerud and Vestfold University College. IEEE System of Systems Engineering (SoSE). Kongsberg, Norway, Sunday-Thursday, 12–16 June 2016.

27. Isaacson, Walter (2011) *Steve Jobs*. New York: Simon & Schuster.

28. Branswell, Helen (2018) "Gates, Trump, and the Flu." *Boston Globe*. Monday, 30 April 2018, p. B9.

29. Ho, Sally (2018) "Gates vows $158m to fight US poverty." *Boston Globe*. Friday, 4 May 2018, p. B15.

30. Jacobsen, Gabriella (2018) "The Disruptive Micro Business – How tiny business can have real positive impact." *Kivo Daily Magazine*,

14 May 2018, https://www.kivodaily.com/finance/business/the-disruptive-micro-business-how-tiny-business-can-have-real-positive-impact/.

31. Johnston, Chris (2014) "Why do corporates give? – What motivates companies to give to charity in cash or kind may differ, but it must be genuine to overcome public scepticism." RCNT.EU/A7K *Raconteur*. 23 October 2014. https://www.raconteur.net/business/why-do-corporates-give.

32. Chernev, Alexander, & Blair, Sean (2015) "You Can Taste the Benevolence – If your customers know You Donate to charity, will they like your products more?" *KelloggInsight*. 7 December 2015. https://insight.kellogg.northwestern.edu/article/you-can-taste-the-benevolence.

33. Porter, Michael E., and Kramer, Mark R. (2002) "The Competitive Advantage of Corporate Philanthrophy." *Harvard Business Review*. December 2002. https://hbr.org/2002/12/the-competitive-advantage-of-corporate-philanthropy.

34. Boitnott, John (2015) "4 Ways Your Company Benefits From Giving Back." *Entrepreneur*. 27 January 2015, https://www.entrepreneur.com/article/241983.

35. Preston, Caroline (2016) "The 20 Most Generous Companies of the Fortune 500." *Fortune*. 22 June 2016, http://fortune.com/2016/06/22/fortune-500-most-charitable-companies/.

36. Coca-Cola (2018) Coca-Cola Foundation. 31 May 18. https://www.coca-colacompany.com/our-company/the-coca-cola-foundation.

37. Starbucks (2018) Starbucks Foundation. 31 May 2018. https://www.starbucks.com/responsibility/community/starbucks-foundation.

38. Sorkin, Andrew Ross (2018) "BlackRock's Message: Contribute to Society, or Risk Losing Our Support." *New York Times*. 15 January 2018. https://www.nytimes.com/2018/01/15/business/dealbook/blackrock-laurence-finkletter.html?rref=collection%2Fbyline%2Fandrew-ross-sorkin&action=click&contentCollection=undefined&region=stream&module=stream_unit&version=latest&contentPlacement=15&pgtype=collection.

39. Albright, Madeleine, with Woodward, Bill (2020) *Hell and Other Destinations – A 21st-Century Memoir*. New York: HarperCollins Publishers.

40. The Week (2020) "A world desperate for masks." *The Week*. 15 May 2020. pp. 36–37.

41. The Week (2020) "Trump's plan to blame China." *The Week*. 15 May 2020. p. 5.

APPENDIX: SURVEY UTILIZED

Website Query

Hello, Sir/Madam:

I'm a private complex systems engineering consultant writing a paper [later: chapter] on humanitarian efforts of important organizations where some fraction of resources is devoted to trying to help solve world problems.

Would you please suggest an E-mail address at [name of organization] where I might provide more detail on this topic and submit a request for relevant information? Thank you. Dr. Brian E. White: bewhite71@gmail.com; (978) 443–3660; mobile: (617) 893–9542; www.cau-ses.net.

E-Mail Request

Dear Sir/Madam:
I have learned good things about your organization and have already explored your website.

This is a request for some basic information in support of a planned paper [chapter], entitled:
Leading Change Management in Allocating More Resources Toward Addressing Complex and Pressing World Issues
with the following Abstract:

Most profit-making companies and other enterprises could do better in devoting more resources toward solving important world problems without detracting significantly from their primary missions. Their leaders should endeavor to convince key stakeholders of the virtues of such actions and the associated public-relations benefits that could well lead to increased business. Leaders and managers should psychologically and materially reward their employees for volunteering their expertise and time appropriately, depending on particular humanitarian target goals. This paper [chapter] makes a case for these premises and shows how complex adaptive systems engineering, leadership, and management principles can enable progress within various complex system domains exhibiting critical situations where many constituents are demanding solutions.

In essence, this paper [chapter] is about urging individuals within organizations, e.g., companies, societies, enterprises, etc., to work with their leaders to ensure that each organization meets its social responsibilities in helping to make the world a better place in terms of improving everyone's quality of life. This can only be done if we somehow marshal more available corporate and other private or public resources to address critical humanitarian problems. An excellent definition social responsibility appears in Wikipedia along with several citations and/or references.

Social responsibility is an ethical framework [that] suggests that an entity, be it an organization or individual, has an obligation to act for the benefit of society at large. Social responsibility is a duty every individual has to perform so as to maintain a balance between the economy and the ecosystems. ... [and] sustaining the equilibrium between the two. [This] pertains not only to business organizations but also to everyone whose [actions impact] the environment. This responsibility can be passive, by avoiding engaging in socially harmful acts, or active, by performing activities that directly advance social goals. Social responsibility must be intergenerational since the actions of one generation have consequences on those following.

Businesses can use ethical decision making to secure their businesses by making decisions that allow for government agencies to minimize their involvement with the corporation. ... "self-regulation" rather than market or government mechanisms ... According to some experts, most rules and regulations are formed due to public outcry, which threatens profit maximization and therefore the well-being of the shareholder, and that if there is not an outcry there often will be limited regulation.

Some critics argue that corporate social responsibility (CSR) distracts from the fundamental economic role of businesses; others argue that it is nothing more than superficial window-dressing, or "greenwashing"; others argue that it is an attempt to pre-empt the role of governments as a watchdog over powerful corporations though there is no systematic evidence to support these criticisms. A significant number of studies have shown no negative influence on shareholder results from CSR but rather a slightly negative correlation with improved shareholder returns.

https://en.wikipedia.org/wiki/Social_responsibility

Taking the first paragraph above as the fundamental truth, the subject paper [chapter] will also explore some aspects of the second and third paragraphs in an attempt to help determine the extent to which exercising one's social responsibility is beneficial or harmful to business. A number of example instances, mini case studies, will be discussed that test the latter premise. Two interesting questions would be: 1) Have government responses to social responsibility efforts led to any reduction in regulations? and 2) Have any public responses to social responsibility efforts been forthcoming that have enhanced organizational business objectives and their profits?

In an attempt to elicit some relevant responses from organizations pursuing some aspects of social responsibility, a simple survey will be explained, and any results received from these organizations will be analyzed and evaluated.

Thus, I would greatly appreciate your thoughts on the above, and if you are willing, some relevant information about your organization, including some quantitative data, that might bolster or refute the premises. A simple spreadsheet is attached which could be completed and returned to me, hopefully, as soon as practicable.

Thank you very much for considering this request. I would hope that your potential response will not take much effort on your part. If you do respond, please indicate whether the name of your organization may be used, or whether I need to keep the information anonymous. I will certainly comply with your preference. I will also share my draft paper [chapter] with you for comment once it is prepared for possible publication. It is [was] targeted for the 39th International Annual Conference of the American Society for Engineering Management (ASEM) to be held in Coeur d'Alene, Idaho, 17–20 October 2018.

[This work is now to be part of a new book, authored by yours truly, below, tentatively entitled, *Toward Solving Complex Human Problems — Techniques for Increasing Our Understanding of What Matters in Doing So*, to be published in the book series (I am co-editor along with Paul Garvey of The MITRE Corporation), Complex and Enterprise Systems Engineering Series, with Taylor & Francis/CRC Press.]

Brian E. White, PhD
Principal, CAU-SES (Complexity Are Us – Systems Engineering Strategies)
(www.cau-ses.net)
215 Mossman Road
Sudbury, MA 01776
(978) 443–3660
mobile: (617) 893–9542

Index